SUCCESS AT WORK

A PRACTICAL GUIDE FOR SUCCEEDING AT WORK

DR. MAXWELL UBAH

Copyright © by 2024 Dr. Maxwell Ubah

All rights reserved. This book or any of its portion may not be reproduced or transmitted in any means, electronic or mechanical, including recording, photocopying, or by any information storage and retrieval system, without the prior written permission of the copyright holder except in the case of brief quotations embodied in critical reviews and other noncommercial uses permitted by copyright law.

Printed in the United States of America
Library of Congress Control Number: 2024925668
ISBN: Softcover   979-8-89518-637-4
           e-Book   979-8-89518-638-1
Published by: WP Lighthouse
Publication Date: 11/26/2024

To buy a copy of this book, please contact:
WP Lighthouse
Phone: +1-888-668-2459
support@wplighthouse.com
wplighthouse.com

CONTENTS

Acknowledgements..v
Introduction..vii

Section 1: Foundational Work Concepts

1: The Four Components of Real Work.. 1
2: Six Primary Reasons for Work.. 13
3: Leadership and Work.. 27

Section 2: Fundamental Work Principles

4: Responsibility: Know What Is Expected of You, Always....... 45
5: Excellence: Go Beyond What Is Expected of You.................. 65
6: Attitude: Deliver Excellence With A Positive Attitude........... 79
7: Loyalty: Be Loyal to Your Organisation................................. 97
8: Manage Well Thy Boss.. 111

Appendices

Appendix A: The Proportion of Work and Work-related Hours.. 134
Appendix B: The Spirituality of Work.. 135
References... 141
About the Author.. 143

ACKNOWLEDGEMENTS

This book would not have been possible without the input and contributions of the following people:

- My beautiful wife, Ijeoma, for reading the various versions of the manuscript and giving me useful feedback.
- Fred Allison, for the constant reminder to publish the book and ordering one hundred copies even before I finished writing it. I am humbled by your faith in me and the book.

And to the following business executives for taking time out of their busy schedules to read portions of the manuscript and making very valuable suggestions:

- Achi Innocent, CEO, Real-Yield Capital Partners Limited
- Chike Onyia, Esq., CEO, Zolts Limited
- Idorenyen Enang, President, National Institute of Marketing of Nigeria (NIMN), and CEO, Corporate Shepherds
- Akin Akinfemiwa, CEO, Geregu Power Plc
- Julius Omodayo-Owotuga, Deputy CEO, Geregu Power Plc
- Ifeanyi Chukwuma, CEO, Performance Frontiers
- Oliver Nnona, CEO, Profiliant
- Godwin Ndubuisi, CEO, Omarihouse Energy

- Samuel Nwanze, Executive Director/CFO, Heirs Oil & Gas
- Stanley Eluwa, Head, Human Resources, Bollore Transport and Logistics Nigeria

INTRODUCTION

The world of work is changing. Major shifts are occurring in the world of work that are changing the nature of work, the workplace, the type of workforce, and the dynamics of working. Such major shifts include but are not limited to:

- The widespread adoption of artificial intelligence, robotics, automation, and digitization. These technologies are changing the nature of work, the workplace, and the type of work in many organisations. New jobs are being created and old ones reimagined and redesigned. Today, there is almost no job that these technologies have not impacted over the last decade, and their impact will continue into the foreseeable future. Many postulates that because of their impact, the workforce of the future would be a digital workforce.
- The impact of the COVID-19 pandemic has led to a quantum leap in the adoption of digital channels and the universal acceptance of remote work. Today, as a result, more people work remotely than before. Many organisations are breaking the divide between office work and remote work. Work is no longer defined by a place but by output.
- The nature of the workforce is also changing. Four

generations exist in today's workforce—Baby Boomers, Generation X, Millennials, and Generation Z. While this offers an incredible opportunity to learn from one another, the divide also poses a great leadership challenge—how to manage the various groups to achieve organisational outcomes.
- The rise of part-time work. More people are working for themselves and doing freelancing than ever before. With a click of the button, you can outsource a part of the work you do to someone in India or Pakistan, for example.

However, while the nature of work, the workplace, the dynamics of working, and the skills required for work are changing, there is one immutable truth: organisations still expect their people to deliver on their tasks and goals. The times we are in call for people to better manage themselves to meet organisational goals. Today's workplaces are looking for self-led people who can deliver business results with little or no supervision.

Irrespective of your job role, the nature of your work, and your mode of working—whether remotely or from the office or a combination of both—the principles in this book will help you become more effective at work.

63%
Per cent of work and work-related activities as a proportion of the total number of useful hours in a week
(see Appendix A)

If the average person spends about two-thirds of their useful hours at work and in work-related activities, it means that we spend more time at work than in any other activity in life, including time spent with our loved ones and in religious worship. We also spend more time at work than in all other activities put together.

Therefore, work plays a significant role in our lives; it is an integral part of life and living. But many people hate the idea of work and working. They believe that work is a curse, not a blessing, and cannot wait to get yonder where there will be no more work. Others start looking forward to a weekend of rest from the first day at work. They celebrate every Friday. They call it TGIF—Thank God It's Friday.

But why should we only thank God for Friday? Why can't we have TGIM—Thank God It's Monday? Why can't people be as excited on Monday mornings as they are on Friday evenings? Why can't people look forward to work as they look forward to going on vacation? Why can't people thank God for the opportunity to work and contribute something meaningful to society?

This book will help you answer some of these questions. Work is important. It is one of life's best gifts, and, as you will discover, it is not a necessary evil.

Here are some fundamental truths about work:

- Work forms a significant part of our identity—what we do shapes how we think about ourselves. When people introduce themselves, they usually introduce themselves by their work. They say something like, "I am a doctor, banker, lawyer, engineer, businessman." Perhaps it is the reason joblessness leads to depression and, sometimes, even suicide. Beyond the inability to meet one's obligations, joblessness destroys a significant portion of our identity, our feeling of importance, sense of worth, role in society, and contribution to others.
  - Work has ripple effects. Fulfilment or frustration at work trickles down to the other areas of our lives—health, relationships, and general wellbeing.

- Fulfilment at work begins with recapturing the essence of work. If our work lacks meaning and is devoid of a personal sense of fulfilment, we will struggle with the concept of meaning in life, just as many today are struggling with the concept of meaning in life because their day-to-day work lacks a sense of meaning and purpose.
- Without finding meaning at work, people lack the motivation for work and the commitment to work. What you get from them, at best, is compliance and, at worst, indifference or resistance.
- Organisations should be "meaning-making" institutions in addition to being profit-making enterprises. Of course, profit is essential, but people do not come to work just to make money; they want to be a part of something great and spend their lives on causes that will outlive them.

I wrote this book, *Success at Work: A Practical Guide for Succeeding at Work,* to help you succeed at work. Written in an easy-to-read style, with multiple case studies, real-life examples, and practical solutions, you will find a treasure load of information and wisdom to help you successfully navigate today's world of work.

The book has two sections—section 1, with three chapters, looks at the foundational work principles. It defines work through *the four components of real work* (chapter 1), explains *the six primary reasons for work* (chapter 2), and ends with the role of *leadership and work* (chapter 3).

Section 2 looks at what I call the five fundamental work principles to succeed in today's world of work. It covers such topics as *responsibility* (chapter 4), *excellence* (chapter 5), *attitude* (chapter 6), *loyalty* (chapter 7), and *manage well thy boss* (chapter 8), a critical ingredient for succeeding at work. In addition, I have added two very short chapters for those who want more in the appendix. Appendix A looks at how much time we spend at work and work-related activities, while Appendix B looks at *The Spirituality of Work*.

If this book helps you to improve your effectiveness at work, please recommend it to a friend.

Happy reading.

FOUNDATIONAL WORK CONCEPTS

SECTION 1

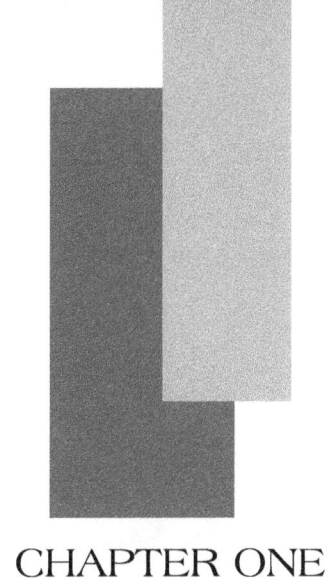

CHAPTER ONE

THE FOUR COMPONENTS OF REAL WORK

> *Jessica is very angry with her boss. She believes that she is very hardworking, but her boss, Jennifer, doesn't appreciate her work. According to her, Jennifer doesn't like her as she always finds fault with her work. She is very frustrated. She is thinking of resigning and has come to you for advice. How would you use the definition of work in this chapter to help and counsel her?*

1

THE FOUR COMPONENTS OF REAL WORK

Trying to define work can be very confusing. Sometimes we feel that we have worked and done our best like Jessica, but we get the feedback that our best is not good enough. We see it every day…

A student writes an exam and expects to ace the exam, only to see the result and is disappointed.

A candidate goes for an interview and expects a job offer because the interview went exceptionally well from her assessment, only to get a rejection letter.

Someone goes on a date and feels that he had a great first date and looks forward to the next date, only to be ignored by the other person.

Do they sound familiar?

In all the above cases, there is a gap between the assessment of their chances and the outcome. When that happens, we wonder what we did wrong? What really happened? What could we have done differently?

This chapter will clear up the confusion about work and bridge the gap between our assessment and our outcomes. To do so, we need to understand what real work is. This understanding will help explain why sometimes our best efforts are not good enough.

When I ask people to define work, I get a variety of definitions, from work as a place to work as a task or an activity, the most common of which is, "Any activity that you engage in that pays your bill." While this definition is a good way to start, it falls short of a complete definition of work and cannot help Jessica address her problem with her boss.

At a fundamental level,

Work = Idea + Execution

Idea requires mental energy, while execution requires physical energy. The centre of gravity of work has gradually shifted from physical to mental energy, which Peter F. Drucker coined as knowledge work to distinguish it from manual work. However, even with the shift to mental energy, we still need physical energy. The knowledge worker still needs physical energy to accomplish her goals.

Therefore, real work requires both physical and mental energy, both hard and smart work.

Real work requires us to expend energy for the right causes, in the right things, and with the right people.

As a basic definition, *work is energy channelled to accomplish your assignment or purpose.*

Real work requires energy that pushes you to stretch to create something extraordinary.

Having understood this basic definition of work, we will turn our attention to the four components of real work.

Four Components of Real Work

One of my gifts is taking complex concepts and making them simple for people to understand. Therefore, based on the definition that work is energy channelled to accomplish your assignment, I will divide the components of real work into four, as shown below. These four components will clear up the confusion about the meaning of work and help many people in the workplace.

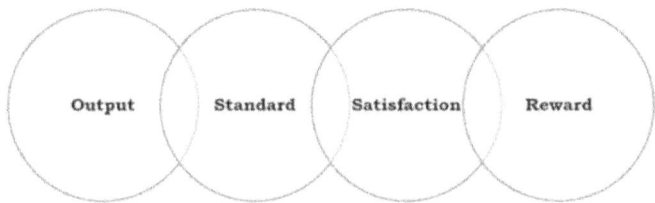

© Four components of real work by Dr Maxwell Ubah

1. Output

Work is always defined by output. It requires you to create or produce something. Without the product, work is not complete. This is perhaps the main difference between working and work. Working is the activity of the worker; work is the output or end result of working. Working can be likened to the process and work as the product.

Work, by its definition, must have an end product. For example, I am working on this book, but I have not worked until the book is completed and published. I am like a pregnant woman; my work is complete only after delivering the baby. You get the idea.

When we understand that real work must have an output, we will focus our energies on completion or execution. Without execution, work is not complete. We might have expended energy, but no work has been done. Completion, execution, and creation are synonyms for real work. Without them, no work has been done. Ralph Waldo Emerson observed that "the great majority of men are bundles of beginnings." They begin but lack the discipline to finish the job. Therefore, the world doesn't honour them as honours are given at the end and not at the beginning. Life doesn't reward people for participating; life rewards people for finishing, as I am yet to see someone win a medal in a race they did not finish.

The first defining characteristic of real work is that it must have an output. Only when we get to the end, when we finish, when we submit our report, only then can we say we have worked. But not before.

Can a doctor say he has worked when he has not seen her patients, a tailor when the dress is not ready, a chef when the meal has not been prepared or a builder when the house is uncompleted?

> *"Real work requires energy that pushes you to stretch to create something extraordinary."*

"It is finished" is the first characteristic of real work. Without getting to the end and breasting the tape, work has not been done.

But output is only one component of real work. Jessica has an output. The student who submitted his script to the examiner has an output. So, what is the problem?

2. Standard

Have you ever sent an email to your boss who informed you that your email did not meet her expectations?

Have you ever ordered a meal that did not meet your expectations?

Have you paid for a product online that you were disappointed in when you received the order?

Many years ago, as part of my wedding plans, I ordered an expensive suit that I saw online. It looked so beautiful based on the picture I saw. When the suit arrived, I was so disappointed that I had to quickly run to a local suit shop to buy another one for my wedding. I could not wear the suit and had to give it out.

Why? The suit did not meet my expectations, the price notwithstanding. It was an expensive flop!

This brings us to the second component of work—work must meet a standard to qualify as work. Output alone is not sufficient to define work as every output is an input for someone else, and it cannot be called work if it does not meet the customer or end user's standard or specifications.

Perhaps this is one significant difference between work and play. Play doesn't really need to meet any standard. But work does.

Standard is the unit of measurement for work. Therefore, a poorly written report will not qualify as work because it will not meet the required standard.

> *"Real work has an output that meets the standard of the end user*

In the total quality movement, defective products are destroyed because they do not meet the required standard, despite the cost incurred in producing them. Similarly, it doesn't matter how long and how much you spent to produce the output; if it doesn't meet the required standard, you have not worked!

In physics, work is defined by force multiplied by distance. So, if the distance covered is zero, irrespective of the force applied, work is zero. Look at it this way: If I tried to push a broken-down truck alone, I would exert tremendous force, but the distance covered would be zero. Have I worked? No. I have simply expended energy. Expending energy is not work if the object does not move. Similarly, expending energy in producing a result is not work if that output doesn't meet the customer's standards.

Based on the concept of standard, people's output can be classified into three:

- *Failure:* when output falls below the required standard.
- *Success:* when output meets the required standard.
- *Outstanding:* when output far exceeds the required standard.

This definition means that you must look beyond your output and all the things involved in producing it and ask yourself: who would use my output, and how would they judge it? Or what is the standard of measurement for my output? Asking this question means you must know the end user of your product and their basis of measurement.

Applying this concept to our introductory case study, Jessica must look beyond her output and look at her work from the lens of her boss. If her boss is not satisfied, then it doesn't matter how hardworking she claims to be. There is something wrong with her output from the boss's perspective. This lesson is important. You do not define work just as Jessica has discovered. The end user defines what work is. And the end user only defines work from the concept of standard and not just output. Their standards become the filter through which every output is judged.

Successful workers start by clarifying expectations. They know that work doesn't begin and end with them. Be like them. Ask yourself, "Who would use my output and what standards must my output meet?"

Therefore, what should Jessica do? First, she should ask her boss what her standards are. And standards have three components:

- *What:* the expected results
- *When:* timing and deadlines
- *How:* preferences and specific expectations.

Then she should go about meeting the standards. And so should you. Never begin a task without clarifying expectations.

In today's world of work, it is not enough to say, "I did my best." The key question to ask is: "Is your best good enough?"

3. Satisfaction

When work meets the specified standard, what is the outcome? Customer satisfaction. If standard represents the rational and objective expectations of the work, satisfaction is the emotional feeling derived from receiving the work.

We know today that people are not just rational beings; they are also emotional beings. And every work leaves an emotional deposit in the recipient, good or bad, whether you are aware of it or not. Your output either increases people's happiness or takes away a part of it.

Just as we classified people into three groups based on meeting standards, we can also classify people's emotional reactions to our work into three broad groups, as shown below.

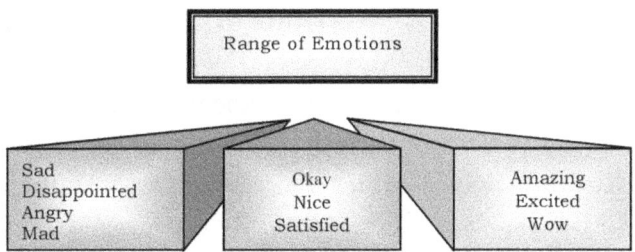

Jessica, your boss is complaining about your work because she is not satisfied with your output! It is nothing personal. She doesn't hate you; she is not just happy with your output. For example, as I wrote this chapter, I took my wife to a five-star hotel to celebrate her birthday. The first time we ate there when they opened, she was elated, but I was satisfied. (Don't mind me, my standards are quite high). However, two months after the first experience, I was disappointed this second time, but she was satisfied. She also complained about the quality of the food.

My takeaways from this experience are:
- There is always an emotional component to work. Cooking, writing a report, playing football, and so on are physical activities with rational measurement scores, but they always impact the recipient emotionally. Take a game of football, for example. The winning team fans leave excited, while the losing team fans leave sad, angry, mad, or even depressed. Rationally, it is just a score (1-0, 2-1, 2-0), but emotionally, it is more than just the score.
- Because most people do not go out of their way to create wow experiences, their customers only deal with them rationally. And when customers do business with you purely from a rational perspective, there is no bond of loyalty between them and the organisation. It is more of a transaction. And transactional relationships do not last.
- Excitement yesterday can turn to satisfaction today and disappointment tomorrow. Past experiences create future expectations. Once a standard has been met, you need to maintain or improve that standard, or you will end up disappointing your customers, and they will leave in droves. Therefore, make it your goal to ensure that your present is at least better than your past. Remember the first mobile phones? Today, those phones will not pass the test, and companies that did not up the ante on their performance have gone bankrupt.
- Never take customers' emotional satisfaction experiences for granted. It can cost you your business. Many selling experts inform us that people buy emotionally and justify their decisions with logic. If you

don't connect emotionally, you will lose their business. Customer complaints, a reflection of their dissatisfaction, can be a rich source of information if we pay attention to them. But if we dismiss them, we might lose their business. For example, Robert, a key account manager in a consumer electronics business, recently got the shock of his life when his most important customer moved his account to another competitor. While disappointed, he noticed that the customer had complained about his organisation's services that he did not take seriously. Now he has lost the customer and his business.

One assignment I give my participants every time I teach the concept of work is this: arrange a meeting with your boss or your most important customer and ask them these two questions:

- On a scale of 1-10, how satisfied are you with the quality of my work?
- What would it take to make it a 10 out of 10?

To add emotional intensity to the above questions, print the range of emotions' chart and show your boss or significant customer and ask:

- How excited are you about the quality of my work or service?
- What would it take to make you excited about my work?

4. Reward

The final component of real work is reward. As defined much earlier, work is any activity that earns you a living. But if you look at our definition of real work, the reward component is the end result of customer satisfaction. The more satisfied people are with your output, the more they would be willing to pay you.

Check throughout history, and you will discover that the

most successful companies and individuals are those whose customers were not just satisfied but also delighted with their products and services. These individuals and companies sought not just to meet but also to exceed their customers' expectations. For example, why would Paris Saint-Germain agree to pay Lionel Messi, a 34-year-old footballer, one million pounds a week, or why would Apple Inc's customers queue for days to be the first to buy and review the latest iPhone?

Both examples might not make any rational sense to you, but it makes logical sense to Paris Saint-Germain and Apple's customers. They know what they are paying for!

So, if you do not like your current reward, what should you do? The answer is obvious: increase the quality of your output! Reward follows output. Ensure that your output meets and exceeds customer expectations. Create excited customers, and life will give back to you in "good measure, pressed down, shaken together and running over."

These four components—output, standard, satisfaction, reward—are the four components of real work.

Having understood the four components of real work, we will turn our attention to why we need to work.

CHAPTER TWO

SIX PRIMARY REASONS FOR WORK

> "Oh, not another Monday again!" Anthony exclaimed. After an extended weekend of fun and relaxation, he wasn't ready for another day of work, not to talk about another week of work. "Why do we even work?" he queried. "Can we not do without work and working? Must I even go to work today? Can they not do without me?" He asked himself. Thinking of taking the day off, he changed his mind and sluggishly and unhappily drove off to work. He muttered to himself, "I can't wait to escape the bondage of work!" Use the concepts in this chapter to change Anthony's perspective about work and working.

2

SIX PRIMARY REASONS FOR WORK

Have you ever felt like Anthony? We all have! And there are many people like Anthony in today's workplace; they do not know the reason for work or have somehow forgotten why they work.

As a peak performance consultant and leadership coach, I have had the privilege of speaking to thousands from the front lines to the C-suites in different countries. During my speaking engagements, I have heard stories of so many "Anthonys". I think they can broadly be divided into three. The first group are those who do not like to work. A Nigerian CEO once told me this story in one African country. He informed me that his people are a peculiar group. For example, someone would call in sick on a Friday and not come to work. But if the organisation is having a TGIF party that day, the same person would show up at the TGIF party, and you would be amazed at their energy on the dance floor. And you cannot sanction them because they are protected by their labour laws.

The second group are those who, although they are at work, are just lazy. They are more like timekeepers and clock watchers. They cannot wait for the closing bell to leave the office. While at work, they are busy with other things not related to their primary assignment. They are physically present but emotionally detached from their jobs.

The final group are those who started with enthusiasm but, over time, have lost their excitement. Work is now just a chore. Perhaps it has to do with the organisational environment or a poor line manager; whatever may be the reason, they need to recapture the essence of working.

I hope this chapter will provide some insights about the reasons for work and help you recapture the essence of working. In this chapter, I will address the following six reasons why we work and should work with our hearts:

1. Work is the womb of greatness
2. Work as the fulfilment of purpose
3. Work as the expression of potential
4. Work as the channel of blessing to others
5. Work as the contribution to society
6. Work as the means to financial rest

1. Work is the Womb of Greatness

Greatness is intricately tied to work as nobody ever achieved greatness outside the realm of work—whatever that work is. I am yet to see someone who truly became great without working. Why? Because every success achieved without working is fleeting at best.

True success can only be accomplished and sustained through work. Do you know anyone of these names: Tiger Woods, Michael Jordan, Elon Musk, Serena Williams, Don Moen, Bill Gates, Jackie Chan, Nelson Mandela, or Mother Theresa?

How did they become famous? By the quality and the impact of their work. Whether it is music, ministry, or medicine, you will only become known when your work announces

"Nobody ever became great outside the realm of work —whatever that work is."

you before your world. As it were, the quality of your work becomes your herald and advocate going ahead of you to speak and campaign for you. And can I say this? Excellent work has no ethnic or religious affiliations or colourations. Whether you are a Christian, Muslim, Buddhist or Atheist, nobody cares as long as you deliver excellent work. Have you ever boarded an aeroplane and asked about the religious beliefs of the pilot? No. You want a competent pilot and not a religious fanatic. Excellent work also transcends national boundaries. Whether you are in Africa, Asia, Europe, or America is irrelevant. What people want in today's workplaces are excellent people.

People become great through work and nothing else. I am yet to see someone who became great outside the realm of work or who became great and said, "I slept my way to greatness." People become great because they work their way to greatness. Although luck might play a part in their success stories, they know how to ride their luck by working.

Without developing a great work ethic, you cannot become great. Henry Longfellow rightly observed, "The heights by [which] great men reached and kept were not attained by sudden flight, but they, while their companions slept, were toiling upward in the night." I like the fact that they toiled their way to the top. It means that there is nothing like effortless success. Success requires work.

> *"Excellent work has no ethnic or religious affiliations."*

Therefore, I see every opportunity to work as a thread in the tapestry of my personal greatness. It is an opportunity to rewrite my success story and create my own luck. And so should you. Running from work or doing a shoddy job is the highway to a life condemned to mediocrity and ignominy.

A healthy work ethic is necessary for success. Mahatma

Gandhi noted that wealth without work is one of the seven deadliest sins of humanity. Don't be caught in that trap. To succeed, you must work. The ancient admonition still holds for successful people, "Six days shall thou work…"

It has often been said that the dictionary is the only place where success comes before work. Successful people know that work is the womb of greatness and the channel through which great individuals are born into the world.

2. Work as the Fulfilment of Purpose

Purpose is the original intent of a thing or the ultimate goal of something. We can also define purpose as the highest utility that a product provides from the manufacturer's perspective. Whatever definition you use is irrelevant. What is relevant is that between the concept of the thing and the production of that thing is work. Work takes purpose from a concept to a product, a mental image to an invention, and an idea to an accomplishment. It is the missing link between vision and its fulfilment, dreams and their realities.

Work is your passport to fulfilling your purpose. It is the medium through which purpose is accomplished and destiny fulfilled.

> *"Running from work or doing a shoddy job is the highway to a life condemned to mediocrity and ignominy."*

No matter what your purpose is, the instrument for its accomplishment is work. Ask any child what they would like to be when they grow up, and you would hear some of the following: doctor, lawyer, scientist, engineer, actor, police officer. But how many children grow up and fulfil their dreams? The jail houses are a silent reminder that many dreams are often derailed and aborted. To dream is good, but we must wake up and work. To dream and not work is to deceive oneself.

I do not know your purpose, but I know that your purpose will not see the light of day or will end as a blighted ovum without work. But when work is infused into purpose, it makes purpose a potent force. Purpose is like an ovum and work, the sperm. When work fertilises purpose, a new creation is born. People who succeed are those who, after discovering their purposes, went to work until they accomplished them. Benjamin Disraeli observed that "nothing can resist the human will that will stake even its existence on its stated purpose." Work yoked with purpose is the secret sauce of greatness!

3. Work as the Medium for the Expression of Potential

Many books have been written about potential, but potential is nothing without work. Just as work is the medium for revealing greatness, it is the channel through which potential is harnessed and converted to skill. Without work, potential dies unexpressed and dreams unrealised.

Your life is like an onion. Wrapped within you are gifts, talents, and supernatural faculties. However, without peeling the onion, you will not enjoy the benefit. You enjoy the freshness of the onion only by peeling and eating it. Admiring it will not do you any good. Similarly, to reveal all that you are and can be, you need to apply yourself to work, to unwrap your gifts for the benefit of humanity.

Was I born a writer? I don't know, but I have written over eight published books and have many more to write. I discovered that the more I applied myself to write, the more I found the grace to write. And the more people think I was born to write. Perhaps it is a gift, but the gift found expression through work. Had I not

> *"Without work, potential dies unexpressed and dreams unrealised."*

applied myself to write even when I did not feel like writing, I might never have discovered the gift and published any book. That is, work discovered the gift, and work is developing and refining it, making it look easy and natural for me. Anytime you see someone operating under an "effortless gift," understand that years of work have made that gift look effortless. Hard work is like a refiner's fire. It refines and purifies talents and produces a marvel for the world to behold.

So how do you discover your gift? Just go and work. Find something to do and apply yourself. We often hear that practice makes perfect; unfortunately, many people want the "perfect" part without the practice part. They want to be good at something without working at it. They forget that a star is simply someone who started and stayed on the track until they were recognised and honoured by their world. Such people want to become stars without starting and staying the course.

Many gifts are lying dormant within you. How do I know so? Because there are no giftless individuals. Everyone is born with bundles of potential and talents. What separates the genuinely great from the ordinary is not talent but work. To discover your talent, you need to get to work. Without putting yourself to work, you will never know how many talents or gifts you have in the first place. Only those who stoop to work will stand on the podium of life to receive the accolades and honours.

Work will not only help you discover your talents, but it will also help you multiply your talents. The more you apply yourself to work, the more your abilities grow. Thus, work becomes the soil, water, air, and sunlight that causes our gifts to sprout and bud.

4. Work as the Channel of Blessing to Others

To understand this principle, we need to take a step back and ask ourselves, "What are the joys we derive from working?" There are so many joys we derive from working, but they can be classified into three.

The joy of completion is the joy we derive from finishing a task like submitting a proposal, solving a customer's problem, or delivering a baby. It is simply the joy of finishing, coming to the end of any activity where we can breathe a sigh of relief.

The joy of reward is the tangible benefit we get for our work.

The joy of end user fulfilment is the joy we derive when the end user of our product is satisfied and even delighted with our work.

The three are essential: it is important to finish, to get paid, and for the end user to be happy with the work done. But if I may ask, "Which of the three is the greatest or most important joy of work?"

If you say the joy of completion, I will ask you, "What if you complete the job and the end user is unhappy because it did not meet their expectations?" You can see that the joy of completion is not as important as the joy of end user satisfaction. If the end user is not satisfied, then your work is not truly complete.

If you say the joy of reward, I will ask you, "What is the source of the reward?" The answer is obvious: from satisfied customers. If you ever get paid for a poor job, chances are you might never be called again to do that job.

True rewards come from satisfied customers. Therefore, I believe that the highest joy we derive from our work is the joy of delighted customers.

Our greatest joy from work is the joy of satisfied customers. If we put money before satisfied customers, we will abort the purpose of work. Is money important? Yes, of course. Money is a great motivator but to put money ahead of satisfied customers is to lose the essence of this principle. It is satisfied customers that will open more doors in the future for you to earn more.

If the greatest joy of work is the joy of satisfied customers, it means that work was designed to be a channel of blessing to others.

Consider the following examples...

A doctor performs a life-saving operation, and people are grateful. Some might even call him a miracle worker.

A lawyer defends her clients and wins a multimillion-dollar payout, and the client is grateful.

A mechanic fixes a troublesome car problem, and the owner is grateful.

A teacher prepares her students for an international examination, and when they pass the exam, they call back to thank the teacher.

What is the lesson here? Our work, when delivered with excellence, becomes God's gift to others through us.

You see, what you owe me in the workplace is not to be my friend. I believe in the power of relationships, but your primary purpose of working or being employed by your organisation is that you deliver excellence at your desk. It is your primary obligation to me.

When we do an excellent job, we give people the opportunity to bless God through our work. The reverse is also true: every time we do a shoddy job, we rob our world of the blessing that God planned for them.

> *"Our work, when delivered with excellence, becomes God's gift to others through us."*

In my book, *The Difference—What Successful People Know and Do That Ordinary People Do Not*, I wrote about the servant who buried his talent. His master called him "wicked and lazy."

Why wicked? I wrote...

"Because potential is given for the benefit of humanity. By failing to develop his potential and deploying it, he robbed the world of the blessings of divinity. Perhaps he would have discovered the cure to a life-threatening disease and saved millions, or perhaps he would have started a business and provided employment to others, or perhaps his books would have given hope to the hopeless. Whatever it might have been, we will never know because he never did allow us to know, and that was why he was labelled 'wicked'".

Did you observe that at the heart of wickedness is laziness? He was called a wicked and lazy servant. In other words, lazy workers are wicked people. Why? They are depriving their world of the benefits of an excellent job!

5. Work as a Contribution to Society

As an extension of principle four, our work is also our contribution to society. When we introduce ourselves, usually with our titles, as noted earlier, we silently inform people of our roles in life and contribution to society. And every society reflects the dominant type of work done in it. According to sociologists, there are four types of societies: tribal, agrarian, industrial, and post-industrial.

The tribal society's main occupation is hunting for food as a group. The agrarian society deals with agriculture and land ownership. The industrial society deals with industries and factories of production, while the post-industrial society deals with knowledge work.

You can see how the development of society is traceable to the dominant nature of work in that society. Therefore, no society can outgrow

> *"Lazy workers are wicked people. They are depriving their world of the benefits of a good job!"*

the nature of work and the contribution of its workforce. At the heart of the growth and development of society or economic renaissance is the type and quality of work carried out by a large percentage of people in it.

One of the primary roles of political leadership is creating an enabling environment for productive work to be done. Economists measure the output of productive work done in an economy through the gross domestic product (GDP). So important is this concept that great leaders boast about the number of jobs created under their leadership and the growth in the size of the economy (GDP).

My work is my contribution to my nation. Through my work, I pay my taxes and my taxes are used to run the country. It is my own way of adding value to the nation. And the more I work, the more my consulting business grows, and the more people I can employ. The more employment I create, the more value I am adding to the nation. This is one more reason I work.

6. Work as the Means to Financial Rest

Everybody wants to experience financial freedom. No matter how much we deny it, we all need money. As some say, money makes the world go round. We need money to meet our basic needs in life.

You see, there are only three ways to get money: begging, stealing, or working. We know that stealing is not an option, so also begging. Why? You can never beg your way to financial freedom because begging depends on the giver's mood, discretion, and goodwill. What is the alternative? Work. The work of producing something for your world that becomes a medium of exchange for the money you want. This is the simplest and most fundamental definition of money—the medium of exchange for goods and services. It means that you must have something to give to your world to get the money you want. Begging and stealing fail in this regard; they take away without giving anything back in return.

Hidden in this lesson is that only creators experience true financial rest. Consumers will always be at the mercy of creators. Examine the lives of the most successful and wealthy people, and you will find at least one creation to their names. There are businesses, patents, lyrics, or even books to their names.

A creator thinks of something new to bring to the world for others to enjoy; a consumer searches for the next new thing to buy. Keeping up with consumer needs with new products or services is the work of creators; keeping up with the latest fashion or fad is the primary mindset of consumers. Innovate or produce is the keyword for a creator; acquire or impress is the keyword for consumers. And it is one reason they remain poor. While they want to impress others with their latest acquisitions, the creators are smiling to the bank.

What product, service, or patent will be in your name? What would you create for your world? For your organisation? For your generation?

Someone will be quick to ask, "Must we all become creators? Is everyone wired to be an inventor? If we all create something, who will be the consumer?"

These are valid concerns. My answer is: if you cannot create anything, then partner with someone else who can. Look for the next major trend or big thing and be a part of it. It is one reason we join organisations—to partner with them to render a service to society.

Being part of an organisation is also a means to experience financial rest. We cannot all become entrepreneurs. Do not be deceived by the lure of entrepreneurship and the motivational speeches of motivational speakers. Entrepreneurship is hard work. If you are not wired to be an entrepreneur, do not force yourself to become one. Find a great organisation and join and give your best to it. Some people will work best in an organised environment while others will work best as business owners. Find the one that suits you, but please work if you are working as an employee!

CHAPTER THREE

LEADERSHIP AND WORK

Matthew was recently posted as the new branch manager to help turn around a loss-making branch in a financial services institution. This is his first leadership position. Excited about the new challenge, he started researching the ideas on leadership and how to lead effectively. However, his excitement quickly turned to confusion. With a plethora of conflicting theories about leadership, he became lost. There is no uniformity about the meaning of leadership, its importance, and how to lead effectively. Some authors focused on leadership styles, others on the leader's personality, others on leadership traits, yet others on situational leadership. Where would he start from? How would he lead effectively? Use the concepts in this chapter to help Matthew to lead effectively.

3

LEADERSHIP AND WORK

Leadership! Everyone talks about it, but very few understand what it means and what leaders really do. Millions of articles have been written about leadership and leadership failures. And millions more will still be written. Yet, effective leadership remains the greatest need of the world today. From Africa to America, Oceania to Europe, the world is looking for leaders in the political and organisational spheres. The fall of Afghanistan to the Taliban is a silent reminder that where leadership is weak or absent, nations regress to dictatorship, organisations become kleptocracies, teams disintegrate, and performance comes to a screeching halt.

Leadership is the glue that binds individuals together to a common purpose, keeps organisations competitive, and nations viable. While this is not a leadership book, although I am a leadership coach and have written a book on leadership titled *The Alphabet of Leadership: The A-Z of Improving Your Leadership Effectiveness*, we need to understand the role of effective leadership from its basic principles. Below is a brief history of leadership from my research.

Brief History of Leadership

The importance of leadership dates back to ancient times during the hunter-gatherer era when communities had to defend themselves against attacks from wild cats (and other ferocious animals) and from one another to protect lives and their land.

The leader is that individual who can best galvanise his community to respond successfully to such external threats. He must be able to anticipate such threats and organise his people to respond effectively to them. His success or failure is measured by the safety and prosperity of his community. The ability to help his community deal with the threats successfully is what defines him as a leader.

Although we are no longer in the hunter-gatherer era, the same fundamental leadership principle is still relevant today. The leader must deal with the threats facing his nation, organisation, or team. His success or failure is judged through the lens of the success or failure of his people. He is not defined by his position or power but by his organisation's performance.

To effectively lead, the leader must have a good understanding of the challenges facing his people—be it an organisation, state, or nation—and be able to marshal the people and resources to respond appropriately to those threats. Any individual who cannot understand the challenges facing his people or lacks the willpower to marshal the resources to deal decisively and strategically with those threats is not fit to lead!

The Context of Leadership

Leadership always exists in a context, and if you miss the context, you miss the essence. From the brief history of leadership, you see that the context of leadership is WORK. Leaders are necessary to help people solve a problem that they cannot solve themselves. In this case, the threats from wild animals or competitors.

Leadership is about producing results for a group of people

and not about having a title or occupying a position. Effective leaders accept responsibility for a group for the benefit of that group. Solving problems, producing results, and accepting responsibility all point to the same thing: work!

Work is the essence of leadership, and the leader's job is best seen through the lens of work. Therefore, the purpose of any office, whether as a CEO, governor, or president, is to work. Those who cannot work or have not worked in the past should not be given any office to lead.

> *"Where leadership is weak or absent, nations regress to dictatorship, organisations become kleptocracies, teams disintegrate, and performance comes to a screeching halt."*

When someone desires the office for the sake of the office and has no desire to work, that person will either become a dictator (drunk with the power of the office) or a disaster (sleeping while the country or organisation falls). And there are many dictators and walking disasters in leadership positions today!

The purpose of the office is to work. Great leaders have a great work ethic. The only reason they aspire to positions of authority is to work for the greater good of their nations, organisations, or teams. They see the office or the position as the privilege and opportunity to multiply impact—to make a significant difference and contribution in the lives of their people.

So, if leadership exists in the context of work, what is the primary role of leadership? I know many would say that leadership is influence. But I believe that long before leadership is influence, leadership is first and foremost service (or work). Those who cannot serve have no business trying to influence people!

But even if we accept the influence theory of leadership, we need to ask ourselves what the purpose of influence is? Again,

going back to the brief history of leadership, we see three challenges facing the community:
- They cannot see the threats facing them.
- Even when they see the threats, they do not understand the implication of such threats to them. The same way BlackBerry and Nokia dismissed the threat of the iPhone.
- Finally, they understand the threats but have their own ideas about how to deal with the threats. Thus, there is no coherence in their approach.

Imagine a group of people who do not understand the threats facing them or refuse to work together to overcome them even when they know the threats. What would be the outcome?

This is where leadership influence comes in. Effective leadership is about creating alignment for a group of people to share and effectively execute a common vision. Effective leaders help people see the threats (and opportunities), clarify the implications of such threats both from an organisational and a personal level, and help them give up their personal agendas for the good of the team. When leadership influence is complete, people subordinate their personal agendas for the team's interests and work cooperatively to achieve business outcomes.

> *"The context of leadership is WORK...those who cannot serve have no business trying to influence people."*

So, influence is a means to an end. And the end is the behavioural change seen in a greater commitment to working together and achieving a common goal. When we influence people, we move them from ignorance to insight, indifference to commitment, and selfishness to altruism. That is, the fruit of influence reveals itself in people attitudes to their responsibilities and work. They have a changed outlook, changed behaviours, and an increased commitment to their work and the team. As a result, irresponsible and selfish people become responsible workers and great team players who hold themselves accountable for business results.

> *This is the heart of leadership—the organisation of human efforts to deal with external threats or maximise opportunities. Leadership solves the problem of how to organise collective effort to create something meaningful. To organise effort, to channel energy towards some great purpose, to pull in the same direction is the unique contribution of leaders and leadership.*

How do leaders influence people to show a greater commitment to their tasks? They do so by making work meaningful, the working environment conducive, and the worker productive.

> *"The holy grail of leadership is to make work meaningful, the working environment conducive, and the worker productive."*

Make Work Meaningful

The first responsibility of great leaders is to make work meaningful and help people find meaning at work. Work must be meaningful for people to show commitment to the organisation's causes. So, how do leaders make work meaningful?

We now know that people's work can be classified as a job, a career, or a calling. Here is a simple summary:

- **Job**: what I do to make ends meet. It is about pay. I do

not enjoy it; I will not recommend it to others; I cannot wait to get out of it.
- **Career**: I like the prospects of what I am doing—financial, social standing, career opportunities, and so on. I am in it for the long haul and will keep developing myself in it.
- **Calling**: what I do is an integral part of who I am. I feel drawn to the work beyond money or career advancement; It brings me a deep sense of fulfilment because I think my work is socially relevant.[1]

For example, writing might be a job for someone, a career for another, and a calling for others. The difference is not the work but the lens through which we see the work.

What is a calling? Primarily, a calling is seeing your work—irrespective of its nature—as an avenue to be a blessing to others and contribute to the growth of society. While a job focuses on immediate financial returns and a career focuses on the long-term prospects of the job, a calling focuses on the meaning and purpose of the job.

> *"It is not the nature of the work that determines whether it is a job, career or calling, but the sense of purpose and the ability to connect the work to the ultimate goal."*

Without infusing the sense of purpose and calling into our jobs, boredom will result. The elixir of pay only lasts for a short while; the attraction of a career can only sustain you for the medium term. The sense of purpose and meaning infused into work is what keeps people going for the long haul.

Many years ago, I was called to speak to an organisation on *The Purpose-Driven Workforce*. Below is a summary of what I shared with them.

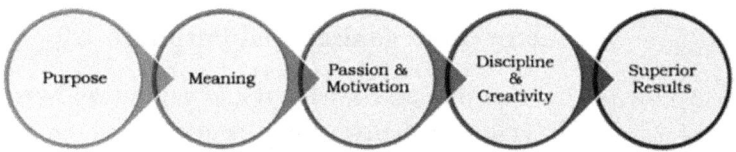

© The link between purpose, meaning and results

The diagram shows that meaning starts with purpose and gives birth to passion and motivation, which ultimately leads to superior results. So one strategy leaders use to make work meaningful is to connect what their people do to the organisation's overall purpose. They start with the why—the overall purpose—before the what—the activity. For example, John F Kennedy, in his "Man on The Moon Speech", started with the why. He described space exploration as the next frontier of the battle between freedom and tyranny, and challenged Americans to take the leadership role as the defender of freedom everywhere. Then he explained the what—landing a man on the moon and returning the person safely before the decade is over. The speech so resonated that in 1962 when JFK went to NASA and saw a janitor carrying a broom, he casually asked him what he did for NASA, the man replied, "I am helping to put a man on the moon."

That's what purpose does. We find meaning not in the activity (carrying a broom, sweeping the floor) but in the purpose of the activity (helping to put a man on the moon). Meaning happens when people can connect their day-to-day activity to the organisation's overall purpose.

Leaders make work meaningful. They have an uncanny ability to help people see the organisation's purpose and connect their day-to-day tasks to it.

Excerpt on Organisational Purpose

Purpose is the unique reason why the organisation was established, the cause that shapes your pursuits and decisions. The best way to answer the question of purpose is to ask, "If your company wasn't established, what would your customers and industry have missed?" or, "What satisfaction do your people derive from working in your company apart from the pay cheque?" Or to personalise it, "What would the world miss if you hadn't been born?" Purpose answers the question of why – why are you in business? Why are you doing what you are doing? Without clarifying your purpose, that is, the unique reason why your company was established, then there is no chance in the whole world that your business will achieve greatness.

So why are you in business? What unique problems were you established to solve? Your purpose is not what you do but why you do it. It cannot be found in your balance sheet or bank account statements. It is found in your heart – the fire that stokes within you, the motivations that get you up every morning to make a difference to your world. It is the why that sets great companies and individuals apart from the also-rans.

Source: Dr Maxwell Ubah, *The Difference—What Successful People Know and Do That Ordinary People Do Not.*

To help people understand the organisation's purpose and connect to them, leaders take a dual approach in describing people's jobs. The traditional way of describing people's jobs is based on the nature of the task or what they do. As a result, titles often reflect the nature of the task—software engineer, accountant, customer service representative, and so on. In the NASA example, the man carrying the broom is a cleaner, and his job is to clean.

Leaders add one more layer. They also help people see and

describe their jobs based on the impact or purpose, which I call the meaning-infused description.

The below examples would help clarify it.

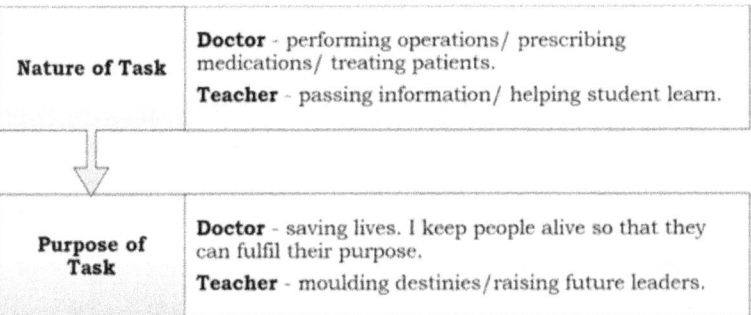

Based on the nature of my task, I am a teacher and consultant. But I see my role as moulding destinies and raising future generations. What keeps me excited is not the information I share in class but the transformation that happens in the participants' lives as a result of my interactions with them. The privilege to help shape someone's destiny and make that individual a better leader is the source of my motivation.

Work only has meaning when we look beyond the nature of what we do to the purpose of the task—the difference our jobs make in the lives of others. This is more than just semantics. Organisational psychologists have discovered that when people reframe their jobs in a meaningful way and the impact of what they do, it makes all the difference in their attitude to work and motivation.

"Leaders help people to connect their day-to-day task to the organisational purpose."

No matter how wonderful it is at the outset, every job tends to become routinised and eventually boring over time. A heart surgeon might be excited about performing his first heart surgery, but by the time he has completed one hundred heart surgeries, the novelty of performing heart surgeries might have worn off. What will keep the doctor excited is if he keeps the view that every heart surgery is an opportunity to save a life and help put smiles back into families. Saving lives is the higher purpose. Operating or prescribing is the task.

For example, as a leadership consultant, I have had the privilege of teaching the same concepts multiple times to different participants in the same organisation. Of course, after a while, the novelty of repeatedly teaching the same concepts wears off. But what keeps me excited is my purpose. The opportunity to help someone along in the quest to become a better leader never ceases to keep me fired up. That's my motivation. That's why I teach. That's why I am excited at every opportunity to speak to people.

Leaders help people discover their why and connect it to the organisation's purpose. And they ensure that their people do not forget the why as they go about their day-to-day activities.

So, take a moment and write out the nature of your task and the purpose of your task. Remember to connect your activity to your organisation's purpose.

Make the Working Environment Conducive

The second thing all great leaders do is to make the working environment conducive. The working environment is the conditions people work under, and it includes the resources and tools they need to be effective, the organisational culture, and the quality of relationships.

It is unreasonable to expect people to be productive when you have not provided them with the tools and resources they need to do a good job or the environment is hostile. In many instances, a critical reason people leave an organisation is the work environment.

The work environment is divided into two:
- *Hard or tangible*: resources and tools like computers, lighting, good ambience, and so on.
- *Soft or intangible*: the culture and quality of relationships.

Most leaders tend to focus more on the hard stuff and less on the soft stuff. They forget that the soft stuff is as important, if not more important, than the hard stuff.

Imagine a new sedan on a bad road with potholes. Not only will the car take a longer time to reach its destination, but if it continually travels on that road, it will become damaged. The hard system of your organisation is like the new car, and the soft system is like the road. A great staff in a poor working environment will not function optimally. The environment, like the bad road, will limit her performance. What is the lesson here? The organisational environment will trump personal genius almost every time. Don't depend on genius to get things done. Create a corporate environment that allows ordinary people to do remarkable things.

One hallmark of a poorly designed work environment is the level of frustration in the system. Because it takes a longer time to get simple things done, people spend all their energies managing the system rather than getting work done. Such a poorly designed system hinders people; it incapacitates their genius. And anywhere frustration reigns, productivity nosedives and breakthrough results become a mirage. So, just before you complain about the performance of your people, check the work environment. People produce what their environment dictates.

Great leaders know this. They not only provide the hard stuff people need, but they also pay attention to the soft stuff—they create the environment that allows greatness to flourish. One of your most significant roles as a leader is building the right organisational context that will attract and allow talent to flourish.

Make the Worker Productive

Everybody wants to win. I believe that one of the primary desires in the human spirit is the desire to win. It is the reason people will do everything in their power to succeed in life, whatever their definition of success is.

Why do we gravitate towards successful people, teams, and organisations? Because inherent in every person is the desire to win. Such people remind us of what is possible and what we can yet become. Their successes become the mirror of what we genuinely desire for ourselves, although we are yet to accomplish. It is one reason we gravitate towards such people.

How do great leaders use this concept? First, they show their people what they can become and commit to actualising it for them. Then they push or stretch their people to become all they can become. As Roslyn Carter observed, "A leader takes people where they want to go; a great leader takes people where they don't necessarily want to go but ought to be."

Show them the picture of their potential, and you will awaken the sleeping giant in them. Great leaders achieve excellence because they show their people what is possible. They communicate to the team their greatness and commit to unearthing the wealth of genius buried inside their people. Then out of their people, many rejected by society, come inventions, breakthrough products, and extraordinary performance.

Great leaders make their people productive. Productivity is the hallmark, the defining measure, and the sine qua non of great leadership. It is why leaders are relevant and why the world needs them.

To make people productive, great leaders provide their people with:

- *Purpose*: they cut through the chase and explain the why.
- *Information*: they clarify the what and how.
- *Resources*: they provide the tools needed to succeed and remove any obstacles on their path.
- *Support and coaching*: they provide the coaching necessary for their teams to meet their targets.
- *Incentives*: they celebrate and reward their people—both tangible and intangible.

FUNDAMENTAL WORK PRINCIPLES

SECTION 2

CHAPTER FOUR

RESPONSIBILITY: KNOW WHAT IS EXPECTED OF YOU, ALWAYS!

> *Mariam is a fresh graduate who has just gotten her first job. The job has everything you can dream of—a leading international brand, great pay, opportunities to work in any of their offices, a great mentoring programme, and lots more. Mariam is ecstatic and cannot wait to get started. She has come to you for advice. What does she need to know to succeed on the job? Use the principles in this chapter and provide her with sound counsel.*

4

RESPONSIBILITY: KNOW WHAT IS EXPECTED OF YOU, ALWAYS!

Whether this is your first job like Mariam or you are a veteran, the principles in this chapter will help you make the best of it.

The first question every employee needs to answer is, "Why was I employed?" This question strikes at the heart of expectations—you were employed to do a job; your first responsibility is to clarify those expectations.

Sometimes people focus on other things and forget the primary reason they were employed. They are like a soldier in an old parable who was given the responsibility of guarding a criminal. He was told explicitly, "Guard this man! If he goes missing for any reason, your life will be exchanged for his life." You would think that someone given that charge would take it very seriously. But he became distracted, and the man disappeared. According to him, "While I was busy here and there, the man disappeared."

Many people are like the soldier—they are busy with other things, and they forget their primary assignment. Then they wonder why life is being unfair to them when they are punished.

At the heart of effectiveness is knowing what is required of you—for example, guard this prisoner, grow the deposit, increase profitability. Everything successful people do revolves around this knowledge. Their effectiveness is not a function of their personalities or leadership styles but a function of knowing what is expected of them. Then they modify their leadership styles and their modes of working to suit the expectations and jobs-to-be-done.

This first principle states that effectiveness, whether as a leader or an employee, is impossible without clarifying your roles and responsibilities. Remember our four-part component of work? If you do not understand the concept of standard or expectations, then output means nothing.

Succeeding at work begins with clarifying expectations and taking responsibility for them.

Responsibilities or Results Areas

Your responsibility is your assigned task, while results point to the satisfactory completion of the task from the end user's perspective.

Let's take a new gardener, for example. His responsibility is to take care of the garden, and the results expected from him are spelt out by the words *to tend* and *to guard* the garden.

Your first job might be as a doctor, lawyer, banker, chef, or teacher. It makes no difference. The same principle applies—you are supposed to attend to your patients, clients, customers, or students.

At a fundamental level, to tend means to take care of something. It also means to cultivate and manage the operations of something. To put it another way, tending a garden means making it better—more beautiful and valuable.

Key Lesson: Your organisation is your garden. Irrespective of your title and role, your primary responsibility is to make your workspace better and more valuable. It is to make life easier and memorable for your colleagues and customers; to make the person who gave you the job say, "I made the right choice."

When people do not understand the simple concept of

tending, their fields become overgrown, their skills obsolete, and their products irrelevant, resulting in poverty.

We are all managers of our gardens irrespective of our titles. A driver manages the car; a doctor manages her patients; a teacher manages her students. We are all managers, but do we all manage well? Do we tend our gardens well?

Ask

To understand the concept of tending, ask yourself the following questions:

- Why was I employed?
- What am I paid to do?
- What am I responsible for?

Never confuse busyness with productivity. Busyness is measured by the clock, productivity by the result. It is not enough to be busy; everyone is. The soldier in our example was. But not everyone is productive. Therefore, the critical question we should ask ourselves is, "Busy doing what?"

Successful people know what is expected of them—by whom, when, and how. They are clear about their roles, responsibilities, and expectations.

In clarifying expectations, remember that no job should have more than three to five major expectations. If a job has more than five expectations, then there is something wrong with the job design. For example, the expectation is straightforward for most football coaches: win the league, qualify for the Champions League or Europe, or avoid relegation. Every other thing is secondary. To meet their major objective, the coaches have to choose their style of play, study their opponents, decide which players to use per game, train and develop the players. But all these activities are geared towards their one big objective. That's the score that matters.

Similarly, what is the one big goal or the most important objective of your job? If, for example, your most important objective is to avoid relegation, continuing with the football analogy, then it doesn't matter if you played attractive football or developed young talents; if you are relegated, you are still a failure!

In 1962, Clare Boothe Luce, one of the first women to serve in Congress, told John F Kennedy that "a great man is one sentence."

One big objective. One sentence. Different words, but same concept.

You cannot succeed in the world of work or in life if you do not know the most important objective of your work. If you do not know your one big objective or are not sure, then ask your boss. Don't assume, ask! Wisdom is asking the people who have given us their gardens to tend what their expectations are—what exactly they want, how they want it, and when they want it. Once you clarify the one big objective, use it as a filter for the other activities you are engaged in.

> *"Successful people clarify expectations, failures work with assumptions."*

Your success in the workplace is not measured by what you have done but what you have done compared to what you are supposed to do. Expectations, therefore, are the filter through which efforts are measured and judged. Without clarifying expectations, you most likely will not accomplish true success.

To clarify your responsibilities, used my TEND acronym. You can never go wrong with it!

TEND

Tasks assigned to you
Expectations of your bosses or significant end users
Needs you must satisfy within an organisational context
Deliverables and deadlines you must meet

Responsibility: The Price of Greatness

People do not stumble into greatness; they become great by taking responsibility for their assignments. Winston Churchill called responsibility the price of greatness.

The case of two servants of an ancient emperor exemplifies the role of responsibility in promotion and success. The emperor was angry with both servants—the chief butler and the chief baker. As a result, they were imprisoned.

While in prison, they both had a dream and hidden in their dreams is the universal principle of responsibility and success.

Hear the chief butler explain his dream:

*"Behold, in my dream a vine was before me, and in the vine were three branches; it was as though it budded, its blossoms shot forth, and its clusters brought forth ripe grapes. Then the emperor's cup was in my hand; and I **took** the grapes and **pressed** them into the emperor's cup, and **placed** the cup in emperor's hand."*

Did you notice the specific words that the chief butler used?
I took…I pressed…I placed.

Action words. Because he took responsibility for his office, he was restored.

Restoration is the end result of accepting responsibility for one's position. When you accept responsibility for the cup in your hand, the assignment your organisation has placed in your hand, it's just a matter of time before you are lifted, restored, or promoted. Life will move you out of the dungeon and bring you back to your rightful place because responsible people are not meant for the dungeons; they are needed in the palaces and the C-suites.

Then we come to the next servant, the chief baker.

"I also was in my dream, and there were three white baskets on my head. In the uppermost basket were all kinds of baked goods for my emperor, ***and the birds ate them out of the basket on my head.****"*

What did you notice about this servant?

He allowed the birds to eat the food that belonged to his emperor. Wow! What a lazy servant. He failed to tend and guard his garden. How could you allow birds to eat the food meant for your emperor? Similarly, how could you allow competitors to enter your market segment and erode your market share without putting up a fight? How could you forget to submit that multimillion-dollar bid that you missed the deadline?

What was the chief baker's reward? He was hanged. Now someone would say that life is not fair because one was restored and the other hanged. Another person would say that the chief butler was lucky or favoured. And yet another would say that the emperor was a wicked leader. But the bottom line, the underlying principle of success and even of luck or favour, is responsibility.

Was it favour that restored the chief butler? No. Responsibility did!

Did the emperor prefer him to the chief baker? No. He created his own success story through the principle of responsibility.

Was life unfair to the chief baker that he was hanged? No. He got the reward for his irresponsible behaviour.

From this parable, we see that the governing principle of the universe is responsibility. When we don't understand this principle, we attribute success or failure to external factors. We forget that life favours no one; we reap what we sow.

Did luck make Jeff Bezos one of the richest men in the world?

Did luck help Serena Williams win twenty-three singles grand slam titles?

Well, luck might have played a part, but nobody ever wins a tournament, comes out with a first-class, or builds a multibillion-dollar business on luck or favour alone.

Responsibility is the governing principle of the universe. Our results follow our sense of duty and responsibility. Responsibility is the door we must pass through to favourable futures and opportunities. Responsible people find that life usually smiles at them at critical junctures with favourable opportunities. Some call it luck, others call it favour, but the fulcrum upon which luck or favour revolves is responsibility. How do I know so? When an irresponsible person is given a break in life, their lack of responsibility will destroy their chances.

Based on the dreams of the two servants, people can be divided into two: those who take responsibility for their future and those who allow the birds to eat away their future.

> *"Nobody ever wins a tournament, comes out with a first-class, or builds a multibillion-dollar business on luck or favour alone."*

Which category do you belong to? Will you sleep through life, or will you wake up and take responsibility for your assignment and future?

Are you sleeping at work or attending and guarding your garden?

One Quick Test of Responsibility: Fruitfulness

The first test of responsibility is to be fruitful. Fruitfulness is wired into nature and is a part of our DNA. In the workplace, fruitfulness deals with productivity. It can also be seen in making a profit over and above your cost of capital. It is ensuring that as an employee, you not only cover the cost of your salary every month but also make a profit for your employer.

Profit is the language and lifeblood of business. Without it, there will be no capital accumulation to employ new people, replace depreciating equipment, and even pay your salaries in the future.

If profit is the lifeblood of business, productivity is the access key to profitability. It is not enough to go to work every day, we must constantly ask ourselves:

- Am I productive?
- What is my contribution to the success of my company?
- Is my organisation deriving value from my presence?
- How can I be more fruitful or productive?
- How can I make a difference today?

No employer would retain an unproductive staff. An employer will only keep you because they are earning far more than they are paying you. When they start to earn less than what they are paying you, they will reconsider your employment. Therefore, be fruitful!

The Responsible Worker

Now that you know what responsibility is, below are a set of attributes of responsible workers:

- Ownership Mindset
- Vision

- Focus
- Discipline
- Time Management

a.   Ownership Mindset

Responsible people have an ownership mindset. They see themselves as owners of their workspaces. They know that they are not just employees but shareholders and critical stakeholders of their organisations.

When your organisation employed you, it took a risk on you. Owning your job and discharging your duties effectively is your obligation to your organisation for taking a risk on you.

Without developing an ownership mindset, you will never be fully committed to your work. If the business you are in were your business, how would you behave? If it were your father's business, how would you act? If you knew that you were being prepared to take over the business, what level of commitment would you give?

One question I ask participants every time I teach this concept is this: if you were to start your own business, would you employ your kind of person? If your staff puts in your current level of commitment, would you be happy with that person?

That's what ownership is all about. When you develop this mindset, you work as if it were your own business. You know that life is testing you before promoting you; if you cannot commit to another person's business, life will not give you your own breakthroughs.

I often remind participants in my classes that you work in an organisation, but you work for yourself. This slight change makes all the difference. When you think you are working for someone, you might not be fully committed. But if you believe that you are working for yourself in an organisation, it makes all the difference. Such people know that life will always reward them for their efforts, whether from their organisations or not. Therefore, their commitment to their tasks is exceptional. They work as if they own the business.

The story is told of an elderly carpenter who was about to retire. He told his master that he was about to retire. But the master asked him for one last favour—to build a house. Because his heart was no longer in it, he used shoddy materials. When he finished and handed over the key to the employer, the employer thanked him and gave the key back to him and said, "This is my gift to you."

> *"Profit is the language and lifeblood of business."*

He was shocked! If only he knew that he was building his own house, he would have used the most expensive materials and done a great job. And so it is with us; we randomly build our lives and then turn back and blame society. If only we knew that we were building our futures with every action we take, we would act differently.

Owners have a way of looking at their businesses: they take a long-term view of the business, see the whole picture, take the initiative, make sacrifices for the business to succeed, and go the extra mile to deliver on expectations. Develop that mindset. It pays!

b. Vision

Vision simply says, "How do you want your work to look like at the end of the day?"

Vision is a mental dress rehearsal. It is rehearsing your day before you begin it. It is deciding the what, when, and how of your day before you enter it. And the better mentally prepared you are, the more likely you will be in control of your day.

Vision is like an architect's blueprint for an expanse of land.

Your work is like that expanse; vision is the blueprint that tells you what the end product would look like.

Imagine people going to a field to build without a blueprint? There will be chaos! Energy will be dissipated in arguments, people will pull in different directions, and the project will be abandoned midway.

Vision is necessary to bring direction and order, and channel one's energy towards building an enduring edifice.

Should vision be long-term or short-term? I believe it should be a combination of both. You can begin with a long-term vision and break it down into short-term goals. So, how would you like your work to look in another five years? Two years? One year? Next quarter? Next month? Today?

Always start your day with a plan!

c. Focus

Remember the story of the soldier who was so busy that he forgot his primary assignment? That's one difference between successful people and ordinary folks. Successful people share an uncanny trait—they do not dissipate their energies in frivolities. They know what matters to them and focus their energies on activities that would yield the greatest value.

Successful people know that their most precious resource is their energy and attention. Energy, the resource that creates marvels, births breakthrough innovations, and gives strength to withstand the onslaught from the opposition, flows from our attention. Whatever holds our attention will unlock our energies and determine our pursuits. And if the wrong things grab our attention, we will pursue them to our destruction.

Your results (and failures) begin with your attention. Therefore, without a filter for differentiating the important from the unimportant, you are guaranteed to fail.

Since energy flows in the direction of our attention, successful people jealously guard what gets their attention. The foremost psychologist of the nineteenth century, William James, said that maturity is knowing what to overlook. I like the quote and would replace maturity with wisdom. Hence, wisdom is knowing what to overlook.

Successful people know that not everything that calls for their attention needs their attention. They live by the mantra, "What I give attention to grows; what I take attention from dies." If you keep focusing on the wrong things, that thing will grow and crowd your life.

To focus on the main thing, to keep the main thing the main thing as Stephen Covey observed, is the hallmark of successful people. Fools and failures are easily distracted. They end up sacrificing the most important things in their lives because they couldn't separate the urgent from the important.

Successful people ask one question: If I give my attention to this person or activity, how would it make me a better person or help me achieve my goals today, tomorrow, or in the future?

Focus is impossible without knowing what is important. That is, priorities drive focus. Therefore, successful people constantly ask themselves, "What are the top three activities that will enable me to achieve my results today?" Once they find those activities, they concentrate their energies until they accomplish their goals.

Some years ago, I wrote an article titled *Seven Wisdom Lessons from Pregnancy*. In it, I enumerated seven universal lessons pregnancy teaches us about success. Principle two, on the concept of single-minded focus, is relevant here. Below is the excerpt.

The very concept of pregnancy is what I call "one baby at a time." On very rare occasions, we see two or more babies at once. (The average rate of multiple births in the global society is below five per cent. Still relatively small compared to single births).

What is the lesson here? It is the principle of single-minded focus on a particular goal until it is accomplished. The attraction of multitasking is a fad. Several studies have shown that focusing on one task at a time results in greater productivity with less mental energy consumption and fatigue than multitasking.

Wise people understand this concept. They know that just like a pregnant woman, they can only focus on one task at a time. (Note: Just as survival rate reduces with a greater number of babies in the womb, the greater the number of tasks, the less efficient and effective a leader will be).

Greatness has within it the singularity of focus. Successful people know the one thing they need to do, when and how. They know that genius is dissipated, energy wasted, and excellence impossible with divided attention. A distraction might sound enticing, but it strangulates creativity as creativity requires single-minded focus.

Just like a pregnant woman, finish one thing before moving on to the next thing. The idea of finishing the first task will give you a sense of accomplishment and provide you with the fuel to take on the next task.

You are more effective when you remember what I call "one baby at a time" or "one task at a time." One task carried to completion is more important than ten tasks that you did not finish.

d.   Discipline

Let's face it: sometimes we don't feel like going to work; at other times, we want to call it a day and go home as we are in no mood to put in the extra hours to deliver a good job. You are not alone. Every successful person will eventually get to the point when they feel like quitting and calling it off. But the difference is that they refuse to quit.

They subordinate how they feel to what needs to be done. They follow through. They hold on and hang on. They do what is necessary even when it is not convenient. Their sense of necessity overrides the desire for convenient living.

Show me a man who lives by the convenient mentality, and I will show you someone who will not succeed in life. Why? Nothing great has ever been accomplished without discipline. No ark built, garden tilled, or Niagara harnessed without discipline.

What is discipline?

It is putting yourself under a yoke to do what needs to be done irrespective of how you feel.

It is subordinating your feelings to your convictions and values.

It is following the narrow path of responsibility even when the whole world laughs at you and scorns you.

Discipline is the IP of successful people, where I stands for **intensity** and P for **persistence.** Disciplined people bring their energies to bear on a task and persist until it is accomplished.

> *"Greatness has within it the singularity of focus... They know that genius is dissipated, energy wasted, and excellence impossible with divided attention."*

Discipline is seen in sweat and blood, in aching muscles and tired limbs, in sighs and groans.

Discipline is having a reason to continue when your body is screaming 'STOP'.

Discipline is wanting to give up but deciding to take just one more step, and then another step, and yet another step until you cross the finish line and can breathe a sigh of relief that "it is finished."

Discipline is pain but pain with a reason. Motivational speaker and bestselling author Jim Rohn noted that there are two types of pain in life—the pain of discipline and the pain of regret. While the pain of discipline weighs ounces, the pain of regret weighs tons.

Discipline is good pain. While it is not necessarily pleasurable at the outset, it yields pleasurable results in the end. But if we run away from the pain of discipline today, we will bear the pain of regret tomorrow.

Successful people submit themselves to the pain of discipline in order to avoid the pain of regret. An African adage says, "When you see an old man carrying heavy luggage on his head, ask him what he did with his youth." Good question. Discipline is doing something now so that nobody would ask you what you did with your youth.

Avoid the pain of regret. Submit to the yoke of discipline. Adopt the mindset of successful people. They stop at nothing until the work is completed and the goals accomplished.

e. Time Management

Focus and discipline ultimately are seen in how you manage your time. Show me how you use your time, and I can predict your outcomes. There are many books on time management, and I dedicated a chapter to the concept in *The Difference—What Successful People Know and Do That Ordinary People Do Not*. However, what is important here is to understand and apply the concept of T-I-M-E that I developed and wrote in the book. The concept simply says that you can classify every one of your activities into three categories:

Classification	Definition
Investment	Investment activities compound over time and help you achieve your goals, whatever those goals are. They are like capital projects; they have a future return on investment. Examples include attending personal development seminars, coaching subordinates, spending time with your loved ones, learning a new skill, prospecting new customers, and so on. You get the idea.
Maintenance	Maintenance activities do not necessarily help you achieve your goals, but without them, it will be difficult to pursue those goals. Maintenance activities, for example, eating, sleeping, and relaxation, are necessary to replenish your energy levels so that you can continue the pursuit of your dreams. However, on their own, they will not help you become a great dad, a great boss, or a great spouse.
Expense	As the name implies, expense activities are activities that prevent you from achieving your goals. They are energy-sapping activities and include things like petty quarrels, gossips, watching excessive TV programmes, being on social media when you are supposed to be working, texting and driving at the same time and so on. You can add to the list.

The concept of T-I-M-E is that at any point in time in life, you are engaged in only one of three activities: I—Investment; M—maintenance; E—Expense. Right now, you are reading this book—investment activity.

Guess what? Life only rewards you for investment activities because results are delivered only through investment activities.

The filter to decide what class of activity you are engaged in is this: How would this activity help me become a better person in life or make me more productive on the job?

	Necessary	Relevant to Goals	Rewarded for It
Investment	Yes	Yes	Yes
Maintenance	Yes	No	No
Expense	No	No	No

If I represents Investment activities, M maintenance activities, and E expense activities, what does T represent in T-I-M-E? It is the total quality of your life, and it is measured by the proportion (not summation) of I, M and E. Peel back the layer of the life of any individual, and you can predict their success or failure by the proportion of I, M, and E. The summation of the three will give you 24 hours in a day or the years of that individual's life, but the proportion will provide you with an insight into the quality of that individual's life.

So how do we maximise time?

First, start your day with investment activities. They are the activities that help you accomplish your goals.

Second, bring maintenance activities under control.

Third, reduce expense activities.

Do these three, and you are on your way to greatness.

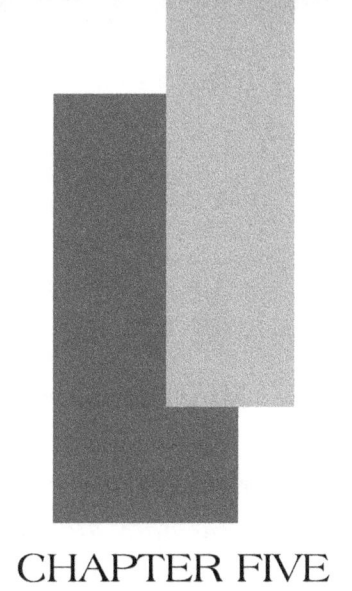

CHAPTER FIVE

EXCELLENCE: GO BEYOND WHAT IS EXPECTED OF YOU!

> *Alexander is one of the software engineers in a multinational IT company. Most of the staff in the department graduated from an Ivy League school. He and a few others did not graduate from an Ivy League school, but he graduated with first-class honours, which was why he was employed. However, those who did not graduate from Ivy League schools are seen as second-class citizens in the department where competition is intense. They are not given critical projects to manage because the Divisional Head, Mr Jones, is afraid of their competence. He has been complaining of late that promotions have been slow because his department has grown so large, and getting noticed is extremely difficult. He has approached you for guidance on how to succeed in his company. How would the concepts in this chapter help him to stand out?*

5

EXCELLENCE: GO BEYOND WHAT IS EXPECTED OF YOU!

The next most important quality necessary to succeed at work is excellence. Responsible people can be counted upon to do a good job; excellent people can be counted upon to do a great job. If responsibility gets you into the game of life, excellence distinguishes you in a crowded field. In today's highly competitive world, responsibility is not enough; we need to go one step further and deliver excellence in our jobs. In today's world of work, it is not just enough to do a good job; we need to do a great job.

What Is Excellence?

Using our four-part work framework, excellence is when your output exceeds the expected standard, which causes people to be pleasantly surprised or delighted by your work.

Excellence is productivity plus. A responsible worker will deliver what is expected of them but will go no further. But with excellence, they will put in the discretionary effort necessary to go above and beyond what is expected.

One of the best pieces of advice on excellence is the age-long admonition that "if someone compels you to go one mile, go with him two." I like the concept of going two miles instead of one. Being excellent has an element of surprise. They expect you to go one mile, but you go two instead.

Notice that excellent people are responsible people. They do what their world expects of them, the one-mile stretch, but they go the extra mile. They add a five per cent, ten per cent or even a hundred per cent extra. That's what makes them extraordinary.

Why Excellence?

There are many reasons for excellence, but they can be grouped into individual, organisational, and national.

- **Benefits of Excellence to The Individual**

The two most important benefits of individual excellence are personal satisfaction and great rewards. Let's consider each one.

Personal Satisfaction. One of the major reasons for personal excellence is the satisfaction that excellence brings. Many people are comfortable with mediocrity because they have not experienced excellence. They live below their potential and hide their talents from their world. And if you truly examine those lives, they do not experience deep satisfaction. Any satisfaction they experience is usually temporary. But once a person experiences excellence, that person will never again settle for anything less than their best. That experience is intoxicating and exhilarating.

If you check the synonyms for mediocrity, you have words like insignificance, ordinariness, unimportance, nonentity, and nobody. Without excellence, therefore, you are insignificant, ordinary, unimportant, a nonentity and a nobody in your organisation. Wow! People tolerate your presence. This is one of the greatest dangers of mediocrity. It robs a person of the feeling of self-respect and the self-dignity that comes from knowing that you are a valuable member of the team.

Excellence is one of life's greatest motivations. People who live by the excellence code are self-starters, self-led, and self-motivated. The spirit of excellence draws them to a higher plane, where they leave the beaten path of mediocrity. While others are content to give up and submit a shoddy job, they will not accept anything less than their best. They do not want their names to be associated with anything less than excellent. They keep pushing themselves until they reach the end of their possibilities. They are exhausted from pushing themselves to the limit but satisfied because they find that the journey was rewarding and worth it in the end. Nothing satisfies them like hearing, "Well done! That was an excellent job! You are simply amazing! Keep it up!"

The self-discovery that comes from knowing that "I can do it" and the self-dignity that comes from knowing that "I am the best" is something they would not trade for anything in the world. It is perhaps the greatest reward of excellence.

"Excellence is one of the greatest motivations there is in life. People who live by the excellence code are self-starters, self-led, and self-motivated."

Great Rewards. Reward is the last component of our four-part framework of work. People pay for goods and services that they are satisfied with. When excellence is your lifestyle, you will receive rewards in two ways—higher premiums and more referrals.

Higher Premiums. When people are satisfied with a product or service, when that product or service exceeds their expectations, they would be willing to pay a higher premium for that service and consider it a thing of pride to be part of the exclusive club.

Have you ever eaten in a restaurant and you so enjoyed the meal that you left a big tip for the staff? Excellence service makes people pay more, and they do so gladly. Mediocrity cannot command a higher premium!

More Referrals. Not only are people willing to pay a higher price for excellence, but they also brag about the privilege of owning that product or using that service. They become ambassadors and advocates of your brand, referring you to others.

Therefore, if there is one decision that you need to make to guarantee success in today's highly competitive world of work, I'd say it is the decision to be excellent, to be extraordinary. Why?

If you are ordinary, you cannot command attention as you will be lost in the crowd. You are a commodity.

If you are lost in the crowd or are a commodity, you can easily be substituted without people noticing the difference or your absence. As a result, your "switching cost," i.e., the cost of replacing you, is extremely low or near zero.

If you can be easily substituted or your switching cost is low, you cannot attract a premium as people will not pay extra for sameness.

If you cannot attract a premium, then you do not have negotiating power, and you are at the mercy of your world. You can only sell your service or product at a discount to guarantee sales, which is a poor and pitiful state to be in as an individual.

Being extraordinary, therefore, is the only antidote to the beggarly state of mediocrity and ordinariness.

I teach people everywhere that money flows in the direction of efficient and innovative products and services. Efficient services can be likened to responsibility while innovative services to excellence. It takes excellence to move from success to greatness.

So, Alexander in our introductory case study, to get the promotion you desire, you need to be so good that your world will not only notice you but also cannot do without you. Excellence is your edge in a competitive landscape.

Martin Luther King Jr. admonished, "If a man is called to be a street sweeper, he should sweep streets even as Michelangelo painted, or Beethoven composed music or Shakespeare wrote poetry. He should sweep streets so well that all the hosts of heaven and earth will pause and say, 'Here lived a great street sweeper who did his job well.'"

Adopt the motto. Do your job so well that "all the hosts of heaven and earth will pause and say, 'Here lived a great (put your job title) who did his job well.'"

- **Benefits of Excellence to The Organisation**

The same benefits of excellence to the individual also apply to the organisation. Organisations known for excellence will command higher premiums and get great referrals.

If you check all the companies in the trillion-dollar group, they are the leaders in their respective sectors—Apple Inc., Microsoft, Google, and Amazon.

Mediocrity has never built a successful organisation. It can build a big organisation, but it will not become a great organisation.

"Excellence is the only antidote to the beggarly state of mediocrity and ordinariness."

Any organisation that does not pay attention to exceeding customer expectations is doomed to fail. Likewise, any organisation that does not enthrone excellence and reward excellence in frontline staff but tolerates and rewards mediocrity in the C-Suite is also doomed to fail.

To guarantee organisational survival, excellence must be the organisational mantra. It is not enough to be big; you need to become the best-in-class in your field or service.

Be known for something. Customers gravitate towards organisations that are unique in a certain area, whatever that uniqueness is. Therefore, find your niche, stake your claim, and your customers will flock to you.

- **Benefits of Excellence to The Nation**

A nation is the sum total of the quality of people and organisations in it. If the people and organisations are mediocre, then that nation is doomed. It will become a failed state. John W. Gardner, Secretary of Health, Education and Welfare under US President Lyndon Johnson puts it this way: "The society which scorns excellence in plumbing because plumbing is a humble activity and tolerates shoddiness in philosophy because it is an exalted activity will have neither good plumbing nor good philosophy. Neither its pipes nor its theories will hold water."[2]

Simply put, when we don't value excellent work but praise mediocre politicians, that society is doomed to fail. And this is the bane of many African countries. We honour mediocre politicians and defend criminally incompetent people either because of religion or ethnicity. And we wonder why the continent is still in darkness.

Where Excellence Begins

Great people know that excellence starts from little things. The attitude they carry doing little things affects their commitment to great things. Ordinary people wait for big breaks before they become committed to excellence. They discover, albeit too late, that when their so-called big breaks come, they are unprepared for them. Imagine a leader who was unprepared for the position he was entrusted with because of party affiliations. The most likely outcome would be a series of executive mishaps and disastrous decisions that would plunge the nation into the abyss of darkness.

Those who cannot demonstrate excellence in little things will not demonstrate excellence in big things. As Aristotle discovered, "We are what we repeatedly do. Excellence, therefore, is not an act but a habit." Excellence is a habit, a lifestyle.

Excellence starts from little things, friend. Your life is the sum total of your moments which are created by the little things you do every day, like the little things you say in a meeting, your ability to notice subtle changes in customer demands and respond on time, your ability to be punctual, and so on.

Excellent people know that the little things they do every day help them strengthen their "excellent muscles" and prepare them for their big breaks so that when the breaks come, they are ready to demonstrate excellence on the big stage. It is like a dress rehearsal. The better prepared we are, the better our performance on the stage of life. We become like David. He was ready to take on Goliath on the biggest stage of his life because he had killed the lion and the bear while tending the sheep. We, too, are ready to shine on our biggest stage because we are prepared.

Excellence and Skill

There is a direct relationship between excellence and skill. Think of the most successful people you know, and you will find out that the common thread that binds them together is that they are skilful people. Choose any field, and you will see that the globally known names are exceptionally good at what they do. Nobody ever achieves prominence with mediocrity.

What is skill? Skill is a learned ability honed by practice that delivers outstanding results. From this simple definition, we see three things about skill:

- *It is a learned ability.* Nobody was born skilful. People are born with raw talent, but talent is not the same as skill. Talent refined through practice is skill. People do not become successful just because of natural talent. Instead, they become successful because they put in the work to develop their talents into skills.
- *It develops through practice and hard work.* Years of discipline is what makes talent look effortless as skill. Therefore, there is no skill you cannot develop, no knowledge you cannot acquire to succeed in life if you are willing to put in the time and effort. Just as practice converts talent to skill, the absence of training and discipline leads to wasted genius.
- *It delivers outstanding results.* Every time we see skilful people at work, we are left in awe and wonder because they make the complex look simple and the difficult look easy. They produce results that amaze their supporters and confuse their opponents and competitors. We may not like them for some personal reasons, but we cannot deny their results. Think Usain Bolt. Michael Jordan. Ben Carson.

Take Cristiano Ronaldo, for example. The debate on which player is the greatest of all time between him and Messi would be an age-long debate. It is such a polarizing debate. Whether you like him or not, you cannot deny his achievements. He has the most international goals in history with 111 as at September 8, 2021. Some of his records on the UEFA.com website includes:

- Most UEFA club competition goals: 137
- Most goals in a UEFA Champions League season: 17 (2013/14)
- Most goals in UEFA Champions League knockout stages: 67

- Only player to score in 11 straight UEFA Champions League games
- Most appearances in UEFA.com users' Team of the Year: 15 (2004, 2007-2020).[3]

He might not be as talented as Lionel Messi, but records don't lie. How was he able to amass such accolades? Through discipline and hard work. You cannot fault his dedication to the sport. He is a testament that hard work will trump talent every time. Someone will definitely break some or all his records, but that individual must be dedicated to the sport irrespective of his natural talents.

You, too, must have the dedication to excellence to succeed in your place of work. Why? If you are average, you are one challenge or downturn away from losing your job.

The only way to truly command respect in your organisation is to be known as someone excellent at something. Of course, you need not become excellent at everything; you only need to excel at something your organisation cannot do without.

Successful people are skilful people. They discharge their duties no matter how little with a measure of skill that makes them stand out.

Developing Excellence

Here are some steps that you can immediately apply to develop the quality of excellence:

Think thoughts of excellence. Excellence is a mindset. You can programme your mind towards excellence by thinking about excellence. What all the ancient sages have discovered is that transformation begins with our thought patterns. How we think shapes what we do. As you think in your heart, the innermost part of your being, so you are. Best selling author

Charles R. Swindoll noted that "the secret of living a life of excellence is merely thinking thoughts of excellence. Really, it's a matter of programming our minds with the kind of information that will set us free." So, start by thinking thoughts of excellence.

Demand excellence of yourself. Excellence is a personal decision. Ted Key, an American cartoonist and writer, puts it this way, "Every job is a self-portrait of the person who did it. Autograph your work with excellence." How do you want to be remembered? Adopt Ted Key's advice: autograph your work with excellence. Demand excellence of yourself even if your world is drowning in mediocrity. Be the spark of excellence in a dark world of mediocrity. Before you submit that project report, ask yourself, "Is this good enough? Does it meet the standards of excellence? What would an excellent report look like?"

Commit to continuous improvement. Excellence yesterday is mediocrity today. Yesterday's niche products are today's commodity products. The only way to remain relevant is to commit to continuous improvement, what the Japanese call kaizen. Successful employees personally adopt the Japanese philosophy of kaizen—continuous improvement—concerning their skills. They look for ways to keep improving the talents life has given them. They practice, learn, get feedback, and do whatever is necessary to hone their skills and make them relevant to their organisations and societies. Join the team. Strive to be better today than you were yesterday. That's one guarantee of success—that you are improving daily in a way that is relevant to your world.

Become a yardstick of excellence. When people benchmark organisations, they are using others as a measurement yardstick. While benchmarking isn't wrong, it is reactive. Why copy others when you can leapfrog them and become the standard for them to copy? Serial innovator Steve Jobs challenged people to "be a yardstick of quality. Some people aren't used to an environment where excellence is expected." And I think we can all agree that he lived his life by this motto. Become the yardstick of quality!

Build in an element of surprise. Everyone loves a pleasant surprise, and excellence never fails to deliver a pleasant surprise. The extra services you add above the customer expectations create the surprise element and the wow experience. So rather than submit a bland report, spend time and design a special report. Add colours, graphs, and pictures. Don't stop where the world wants you to stop. Go two miles instead of one. Adopt the customer service mantra of under promise but over deliver. When you under promise, you give yourself the opportunity to surprise the person when you over deliver.

Monopolise an area. Excellent people monopolise an area of skill. They know something that others don't know. They are good at something that others aren't good at. All the trillion-dollar companies we mentioned found an area that they monopolised. Follow the same logic. What applies to businesses also applies to you. You can go from being a relative unknown employee to the most talked about and dominant employee in your organisation. But to do so, you need to find an area and stake out a claim of excellence. Master an area, a skill, a customer problem better than the rest. Become the resource person and the research fellow of a topic or area. Carve a niche for yourself. Become an expert, an authority in one area.

Solve critical problems. Excellence can be seen in mundane things but to truly distinguish yourself, you need to solve complex problems. When I teach this concept, I ask my participants to picture a hospital. I say to them that there are so many workers and professionals in a hospital like the security person, front desk staff, nurse, doctor, consultant, and so on.

When I ask them who earns the highest, the answer is always the consultant. Why? Because he is a specialist. So how is a specialist different from the average doctor? We go back and forth until we arrive at the fact that the consultant solves more complex problems than the average doctor. We conclude that the rewards of both the doctor and consultant are tied to the nature and complexity of the problems they solve. And same with us. In every profession, the highest-paid are those who solve far more complex problems. While we can all be excellent irrespective of our roles, we need to excel at solving complex problems to earn more in life. The higher the ladder we climb at the types of problems we solve, the more our rewards will be in life.

Begin now. The ancient Chinese proverb that "the best time to plant a tree was 20 years ago. The second best time is now," is applicable here. We should have been taught how to develop excellence twenty years ago. But it is never too late to start now. Twenty years from today, you will arrive. But where—on the podium of excellence or the ash heap of mediocrity? The world needs to applaud you. Start today. Make the promise that you will only be associated with excellence.

CHAPTER SIX

ATTITUDE: DELIVER EXCELLENCE WITH A GREAT ATTITUDE

> *Joshua works in the finance department of a manufacturing company. He is very knowledgeable about his job and also exceptionally skilful. He has all the necessary professional qualifications and expertise, both local and international. However, Joshua is exceedingly difficult to get a hold of and get along with. Every new day comes with a new excuse not to show up at work. And when you give him an assignment, his default response is to complain and argue. As his boss puts it, "He will do an excellent job if only you can get him to do the job and stomach his complaints." The boss is confused. Joshua should be an asset to the organisation with his knowledge and skills, but he is punching below his weight. What is the problem with Joshua?*

6

ATTITUDE: DELIVER EXCELLENCE WITH A GREAT ATTITUDE

Sometimes, life is a mystery. We envy some people because, to us, they have it all—talents, gifts, and endowments. From a distance, we pray to become as blessed as they are. But after a few years, when we hear about them or meet them again, we cannot help but wonder what happened to them. They are struggling to make ends meet or struggling to hold on to a job. We can't seem to reconcile it. Yet, we, with less potential, privileges, and opportunities are doing far better than them. All the potential and promise of greatness they once had had been wasted. What a shame!

Sometimes, like in the case of Joshua, some people have all the knowledge and skills necessary to succeed yet cannot function optimally and achieve their potential because a weakness in their character limits them. The problem with Joshua and such people does not lie in the knowledge and skill domains but in their attitudes—to life, work, others, and themselves. Although Joshua is very skilful, he does not have the right attitude towards his work and to his colleagues.

Attitude Defined

A simple definition of attitude is your inner disposition or internal dialogue (thinking and beliefs) that shapes or governs your behaviours. Your attitude always manifests in your behaviours, but it begins internally. That is, behaviours are the fruits of the seed of attitude. If someone's behaviour is wrong, there must be a problem in the person's attitude.

The below cycle captures the importance of attitude.

© Beliefs-Attitude-Results Pathway

Our attitude reflects our beliefs about life, events, and people. What we believe about life, people, events, and ourselves usually manifests in our attitude. For example, if you believe that people cannot be trusted, it will manifest in a suspicious attitude. You will be very skeptical of people. If you believe that your partner is taking undue advantage of you, you will become overly aggressive or reduce your commitment to the person.

Our attitude determines our approach to life. How we approach life is often a reflection of what we believe. Self-confidence or fear is often a manifestation of our beliefs which manifest in our attitude. People succeed not because they have more talents or opportunities but because they took whatever talent they had and entered the battlefield. And life applauded them for their courage. Others with more talents were afraid of stepping out into the limelight and died in obscurity with so much talent buried inside of them.

Our attitude also affects the quality of our relationships. What we believe about people will determine how we approach them, and our engagement with them will determine their response to us. Just as Newton discovered, their reaction would be equal and opposite to our action. What we get from life is a function of what we give to it. If you want friends, you need to become friendly. If you are critical of people, others also will be critical of your mistakes. Whatever you give, life will give back to you in "good measure, pressed down, shaken together and running over." So, if you don't like what you are getting from life, you need to change your behaviours. And changes in behaviour begin with a change in attitude.

Our attitude ultimately determines our results. If you multiply your beliefs by your approach and the quality of relationships, what you get is the results you created, whether you like the results or not.

Your outcomes ultimately reflect your attitude. It is for this reason many have said that your attitude determines your altitude. You cannot climb higher in life with a nosedive attitude.

What is the lesson here? Enduring success is impossible without the right attitude. While attitude alone does not guarantee success, true and lasting success is impossible without it.

> *"Your beliefs multiplied by your approach and the quality of relationships determine your ultimate results."*

As a simple equation, success = potential x attitude.

Your attitude determines the degree of potential you will harness or express. It is the catalyst of success.

Two Types of Workplace Attitudes

Workplace attitudes can be classified as either negative or positive.

Negative attitude. A negative attitude is an attitude that affects your commitment to your job, negatively impacts your relationships with your colleagues, and prevents you from functioning at your maximum capacity.

Some of the characteristics of people with a negative attitude are:

- *Indifference.* They do not care about the quality of their jobs. You can't get a hold of them to do their jobs, and even if you find them, they won't put in their best efforts.
- *Arrogance and pride.* They feel that they are too big for some tasks. Therefore, they will not pitch in to help their colleagues except if they will take the credit. Because of pride also, they do not take corrections easily. They become defensive at feedback—they defend themselves, dismiss the feedback, or even attack the person giving the feedback.
- *Bitterness.* They are like bile, the bitter greenish liquid. Anything they touch turns bitter. They feel that the world is against them. They find fault in everything and complain too much. They see problems in every opportunity. When they enter an environment, the atmosphere quickly changes for the worse.
- *Sense of entitlement.* They act as if the world owes them a favour. They are very ungrateful; no matter what you do for them, they will never appreciate it. To them, it is their right and not a privilege. They will even turn back and condemn you for not helping them enough.
- *Blame Game.* It is never their fault. They cannot apologise

or accept responsibility for their mistakes. They blame everyone else except themselves. They are too perfect in their own eyes to make mistakes or too elevated in their own assessment of themselves to condescend and apologise to others.

- *Difficult to get along with:* They are high maintenance colleagues. They are poor team players. Like fragile goods that must be handled with care, you need to be extremely careful with them. Troublesome. Cantankerous. Obnoxious. They leave a wake of trouble everywhere they go; they fight with colleagues, customers, and even superiors.
- *Diabolical:* Many years ago, a friend told me something I have never forgotten. He reminded me that putting out someone's candle in darkness would not enhance the brightness of your candle. These people delight in putting out the candles of others because they want to be the only ones to shine. They set up their people to fail. They start a campaign of calumny against their perceived competitor.

"Success = Potential x Attitude."

Positive attitude. The opposite of the negative attitude. People with a positive attitude are incredibly open and warm, easy-going, helpful, willing to go the extra mile for their colleagues and customers. They deliver outstanding results and have good relationships with people.

Attitude and Value

Ultimately, you are rewarded for the value you bring to the team or organisation. Therefore, knowing how to increase your value in the workplace and life should be your primary goal.

To keep it simple but not simplistic, here is an equation I developed to capture the concept of your personal value:

Your Personal Value (PV) =
Contribution Value (CV) – Nuisance Value (NV)

Your contribution value is what you contribute to the team; it is determined by your knowledge, skill, sense of discipline, and other related concepts we have covered. When organisations ask for people's curriculum vitae, they are trying to gauge their potential contribution value. Do they have the required competencies to deliver on the job? Have they done it before? Can they perform when they join us?

But when the people join the team, their nuisance value becomes apparent. Your nuisance value is the inconvenience you cause to the team. Some people's nuisance value is that they complain too much, are very argumentative, aggressive, disorganised, or lazy.

Everyone has nuisance value. Your NV is largely determined by your attitude—how you approach your tasks and the quality of your relationships with people.

Based on the personal value equation, there are only two ways to increase your value to the team: increase your CV or reduce your NV or do both simultaneously. While responsibility and excellence will help you increase your CV, the right attitude will help you reduce your NV, thereby increasing your PV.

Your NV is seen in your ways of working, especially in your weaknesses. Therefore, it pays to know yourself, your strengths, but especially your weaknesses. A lot of people know their strengths but tend to deny their weaknesses. What they forget is that even if they deny them, people see and experience their weaknesses. Denying your weaknesses will not make them disappear. Playing the ostrich is for children. Adults own up to their weaknesses and work to change them!

Your weaknesses are broadly divided into two:

- *Task-related:* those that prevent you from delivering excellence. They are job-related weaknesses like poor attention to detail, lack of numerical skills, poor time management skills, poor organisation skills, poor presentation skills.
- *People related:* those that affect your working relationships with others. They are called interpersonal weaknesses because they are seen in your interactions with others. Examples include poor listening skills, lack of empathy, being too rigid and inflexible, lack of self-control, poor teamwork skills. One of the best ways to find out your interpersonal weaknesses is through feedback. Ask the people you interact with what you do that gets on their nerves or hinders your working relationships with them, and they will tell you if they see you are sincere. We all have blind spots. Feedback brings our blind spots into the open so that we can correct them.

These weaknesses have the potential of limiting your effectiveness and your contribution value to the team. From my experience as a leadership coach, I know that task-related weaknesses are easily fixed by training and coaching. What is usually more challenging is correcting interpersonal weaknesses. Every time we have been called to provide executive coaching for people, they are usually people who are very competent functionally but are being hindered by their interpersonal weaknesses.

Take Michael, an assistant manager, for example. He is aggressive and incredibly competitive by nature. He likes the spotlight and is not afraid of confronting problems or people headlong. The challenge, however, is that Michael doesn't care about people's feelings in the process. He is impatient with people he considers slow learners or who do not see things from his perspective and, usually, it is either his way or the highway.

What is Michael's problem? In his desire to get ahead, he is willing to bully and bulldoze anyone in his way, including his team members. It is an attitude problem. Can he get to the top? Yes. Will he be effective? No. There will be high turnover in his team, low morale, and unsustainable business results.

Guess what? It doesn't matter how high your CV is, if your NV is extremely high also, someday you will be asked to leave the organisation because the cost of managing you and the disruption you are causing to the team is not worth your contribution to the organisation. For example, imagine someone who contributes a hundred thousand dollars to the team but causes five people to leave whose contributions are twenty thousand dollars each. The net contribution of that individual is zero. And if you add the cost of replacing the five people who left, the net contribution is negative. You get the idea.

The right attitude will help you improve your value to the team and organisation. People will not only gravitate towards you, but they can also trust you to deliver an excellent job without micromanaging you.

Three Practical Attitudes to Develop

Attitude 1: Punctuality

There are just a few critical decisions you need to make to succeed in life, and one of them is the decision to always be punctual for meetings and appointments. Why is this important? One way we judge someone's character is by their

ability to keep to time. Think about the following scenarios:
- It is your first business meeting with someone to partner with, and they arrive late with no important excuse.
- Or it is your first day at work, and you were given an assignment, but you submit it two hours late.
- Or an interview candidate arrives late and doesn't have any justifying reason.

Even though we might recover from the initial experience, we have already started on the wrong footing. We allow others to judge us wrongly when we do not keep to time.

Successful people understand this concept—they make it their duty to always be on time for every appointment. If they are running late, they call in advance to tell others. However, this is an exception for successful people, not the rule.

When you are punctual, you communicate two salient truths:
- You inform others that you consider them and the appointment important.
- You are an organised person.

Punctually begins with attitude. Respect people by showing up on time. Make it a goal never to be late for a meeting or an appointment.

The 4 Major Costs of Lateness

Sometimes to appreciate something, you need to know the cost of not having it. We have been told, for example, "If you think education is expensive, try ignorance." So, to appreciate the benefits of being punctual, let's consider the cost of lateness.

- **Reputational Damage**

Your character (C) is who you are, everything about you; your reputation (R) is who others think you are. Although you are more than your reputation, to people, you are your reputation.

My three equations based on the relationship between character and reputation are:

- *Authenticity* is when $R = C$, i.e., what people think you are is congruent with who you are.
- *Celebrity* is when $R > C$, i.e., your reputation far outstrips your character. Some celebrities are drug addicts, sexual predators, and the rest. When such behaviours come to light, we are usually disappointed.
- *Prejudice* is when $R < C$, i.e., people are biased towards you and judge you unfairly.

When you go late for a meeting, which of the three kicks in?

Each time you go late, you allow prejudice to kick in and damage some portion of your reputation. And when people know you are someone who doesn't keep to time, they will transfer that judgment to the other aspects of your life. When people continuously fail to keep appointments, we begin to doubt their integrity. If they cannot honour their commitment to an appointment they agreed to, would they honour their words in other areas?

- **Emotional Cost**

When you are running late for an appointment, anxiety builds up, and the tendency to transfer that anxiety to others makes you aggressive. Sometimes it affects your confidence and composure. Anxiety, aggressiveness, and lack of composure will affect your performance in life.

And if you are running late and do not care or are indifferent, then it is a sign of mediocrity and shows you need help.

- **Financial Cost**

Have you ever missed your flight because of lateness and had to reschedule it? Have you ever missed a bid because you arrived late? There are financial costs to lateness.

- **Missed Opportunities**

Have you ever missed an opportunity because of lateness? Sometimes the price we pay for lateness is a golden opportunity missed. Solomon understood this when he noted that success "is all decided by chance, by being in the right place at the right time."

There is no wisdom in being late. Arrive early and save yourself the costs of lateness.

Attitude 2: Helpfulness

I know you want to succeed and are focused on your goals, but one way to achieve your goals faster is to help others achieve their goals. When you help others, they will, in turn, help you achieve your goals. It is called the law of reciprocity. They become indebted to you to help you achieve your own goals.

Some people are so focused on getting ahead that they are willing to sacrifice getting along with others just to get ahead, like the example of Michael, the assistant manager. They may get to their dream position, but the lack of support from the people they have crushed on their way to the top causes their downfall eventually. Woe to that person who has no one to show up for them on the day of their greatest need!

You should have an attitude that says, "I am willing to help." Be someone people can call when they are in need.

Where Helpfulness Begins

I believe helpfulness begins with understanding one of the primary reasons for work—as a channel of blessing. Therefore, helpfulness is looking for opportunities to be a blessing to someone in the workplace. And one of the very first ways to help people is to do a good job—to ensure that your work will make life easier for the next person is perhaps the starting point of helpfulness.

Delivering excellence is a good start, but you can deliver excellence with a selfish and arrogant attitude, one that says, "Look at me! I am a genius, and you are lucky to have me." This arrogant attitude will diminish your relevance to your team because it will increase your nuisance value. So, add to your excellent job three things: a humble disposition, a kind word, and a kind act.

A humble disposition says, "I am glad to be a member of this great team and happy to contribute my part to help the team to win. Any gift I have is for the good of the team."

A kind word is complimenting someone for doing a good job, giving credit to someone for their ideas, empathizing with someone going through pain. Such words uplift the spirit and draw people to us.

Consider the following true-life story. A lady lost her baby during the delivery process. She called her boss and explained everything and requested a month off. "For what?" asked the boss. She was stunned and responded to her boss, "If my baby had survived, I would have been entitled to three months off." The boss replied, "But your baby did not survive." Wow! Although this happened many years earlier, she teared up as she narrated the experience.

What the grieving staff needed at that time was not someone who would read out the company's policies but someone who would understand her pain. A kind word would have made all the difference. It would not bring back the baby but would help her to manage the pain better. She would have taken solace in the fact that someone understood what she was going through. Instead, her boss aggravated her pain by reminding her that her baby did not survive. As a matter of principle, if you cannot reduce someone's pain, please do not add to it.

Decorum or tact is important here. If you cannot say something nice or helpful, then please, by all means, do not say anything at all. Sometimes keeping quiet is more powerful and helpful than speaking a thousand words! Remember the admonition that "even a fool is counted wise when he holds his peace; when he shuts his lips, he is considered perceptive."

If you must say something, then ask yourself: is it the truth? Is it necessary? Would it be helpful? Is it the right time, place, and occasion? Must I say it?

Let's apply these filters for what the callous boss said:
- Is it the truth? Yes. The baby did not survive.
- Is it necessary to remind her? No.
- Would it be helpful? No.
- Is it the right time, place, and occasion? No.
- Must I say it? No.

The lesson here is straightforward: saying the truth can sometimes be hurtful and harmful if you do not use the other filters to gauge your truth. So, it is not enough to speak the truth; we must "speak the truth with love."

When we use decorum, we not only speak the truth, but we speak the relevant truth necessary for the occasion. Not all truths are relevant! Know the difference and use wisdom appropriately.

A kind act is seen by going the extra mile to support someone in need. Like the good Samaritan, we stop and help people struggling to meet their goals and targets.

There are several benefits of helping colleagues, but I'd like to focus on three:
- *It builds your reputation.* Someone once said that you are either known for the problems you created or the ones you solved. I know which one I'd prefer. When you help people, you are building a good reputation in the organisation.

- *It prepares you for leadership.* Leadership is a one-to-many relationship. If you can start now to be helpful, you are building your empathy muscles and coaching skills—two essential ingredients in becoming a good leader.
- *It leads to promotions and job opportunities.* Because you are helpful, others outside your department know you. When there are promotional opportunities, you have allies and advocates in other departments who will fight for your promotion if your name is mentioned during calibration meetings.

Sometimes the job opportunities can be outside your organisation. Once, while facilitating a class, I was told the story of a bulk teller (responsible for counting bulk cash in a bank) that we would call Steve. One day, a customer came in at about 4 pm with a lot of cash to count. (4 pm is the usual cut-off time for customers). While the other tellers started complaining about when the customer came in, Steve told the customer that he would count his money. The customer was so grateful, and that led to the beginning of a friendship between the two. After that, every time the customer came to the bank, he would wait for Steve. One day, as Steve counted the customer's cash, the customer asked him if he would like to join their organisation and go to London for a one-month training. He informed Steve that an opportunity recently opened in their company for two people, and he had mentioned his name to his CEO. The CEO asked him to determine whether he would be interested in taking up the offer. Steve said yes. The company asked for his passport, applied for the visa, and he went for the one-month training in London. On getting to London, he so impressed the staff that he was

> *"When we use decorum, we not only speak the truth, but we speak the relevant truth necessary for the occasion."*

retained. Today, he is in London working for an international company. But the "breakthrough" started with a helpful attitude.

I have also heard the story of a young teller in Nigeria who served an elderly customer so well that he was impressed by her helpful attitude. The next time he came to the bank, he asked her if she was married. She smiled but said no. He then told her that he would like his son, an American, to marry her. He informed the lady that he had been looking for a wife for his son and believed he had found the right person. She thought he was joking but gave him her phone number because he asked for it. He gave the number to the son. The rest, they say, is history. Today, she is married and living in the US.

Helpfulness pays!

A caveat. While being helpful is a good attitude to develop, pay attention to these three warnings, especially with colleagues:

- *Don't volunteer if volunteering will prevent you from completing your primary assignment.* Being helpful should not prevent you from accomplishing your own tasks.
- *Don't volunteer if you notice that you are becoming a dumping ground.* Some people would want to take advantage of your kindness and pass their assignments to you. Being helpful also has its limits. It is not accepting responsibility for other people's jobs. Only help someone when you are sure the person has a need and not trying to shirk their responsibilities.
- *Don't keep helping someone who doesn't want to learn.* You are actually doing the person and yourself a disservice. If, for example, you assist someone in designing her report, and she likes your job, that does not mean that you should keep helping the person every time to design her report, especially if the person is a peer. Instead, create time to

teach the person how to design reports so that she can do it herself next time. And if the person says she doesn't have the time or is too busy, or you should just do it for her, learn to say no politely. If she cannot learn to become better, she doesn't deserve your time. She is taking advantage of you. Helpfulness, at this stage, means being assertive and saying no politely.

Attitude 3: Smile

A smile is one of the most potent forces for improving your attitude and the overall quality of your life. It makes you look beautiful, warm, and attractive. People gravitate to people who smile. They appear friendly and welcoming. And it helps us to trust them more.

One other benefit of smiling is the calming effect of smiling. Although we think that a smile is a gift we give others, on the contrary, it is one of the most significant gifts we give ourselves. When we smile, we communicate to our inner world that something good is happening, which causes "feel good" hormones to be released, and they help to improve our mood. Thus, smiling is an effective stress reliever. So, why not wear a smile today?

What is the opposite of smiling? Frowning. And I know which one the world prefers. When you smile at your world, the world will smile back at you. When you frown at your world, the world will frown back at you. And just as smiling calms you down, frowning increases stress and tension. Over time, your physical appearance, emotional wellbeing, and results will mirror your dominant facial expression. Those who have developed the habit of smiling will look more youthful, have a better emotional state, and live more fulfilling lives than those who do not.

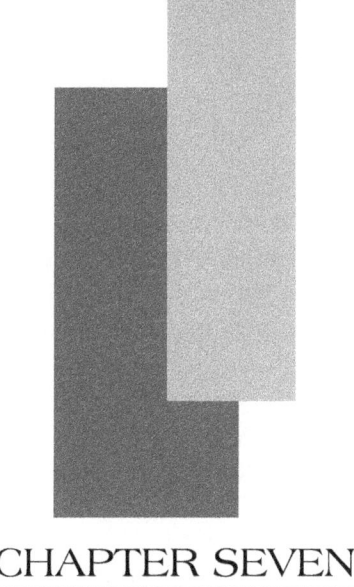

CHAPTER SEVEN

LOYALTY: BE LOYAL TO YOUR ORGANISATION

> *Josephine couldn't understand it. She has consistently exceeded her targets and was tipped to become the country manager of the new country that her organisation planned to expand into. Because her boss, Jude, a senior executive, made a compelling case for her to the management, she was expecting it and had started preparing for it. In her excitement, she told her family and friends that she would be relocating soon. To her, it was a slam dunk case. However, when it got to the board, one member objected. She reminded the board how Josephine held them to ransom two years ago to match an offer from a competitor, or she would leave. What made it painful was that it happened after the organisation had called her to explain their plans for her and sent her for a foreign course in preparation for the new assignment. But on coming back, she brought an offer letter from a competitor and told the organisation that she would leave if they did not match the offer. "We had no choice but to match the offer. If she goes to the new country and gets another offer, would she also hold us to ransom?" she asked.*
>
> *Another board member reminded the board that sometime last year, when Josephine was on vacation, an emergency arose that she was the most senior person best positioned to deal with the situation because of her knowledge of the peculiar circumstances. They requested that she cut short her vacation and help the organisation resolve the issue. She refused because she had planned the vacation for a while. And she was well within her rights to do so, but the board needs senior people that would go above and beyond the call of duty when unusual circumstances demand. "Can she be relied upon to rise to the occasion when such situations arise as a country manager?" She asked.*
>
> *Another pointed out that while she is very analytical and performance-oriented, she doesn't know when to give up and accept a decision not in her favour. "She is too headstrong," was the comment. "She complains about decisions she doesn't like to other divisional heads and team members. As a country manager, would she represent the organisation effectively?" He queried. "If some decisions don't go her way, how would she handle it?"*
>
> *After extensively deliberating her case, the board decided against her nomination and chose another candidate instead. When the announcement was made, Josephine was stunned and deflated. She couldn't understand it as it did not make any rational sense. How would you use the concept in this chapter to help her in the future?*

7

LOYALTY: BE LOYAL TO YOUR ORGANISATION

You are a responsible staff, and you go the extra mile to deliver excellence. You also have a great attitude towards your work. What else do you need? You need one more ingredient, like the icing on the cake, and it is the quality of being loyal. The higher you climb the organisational ladder, the more important this quality becomes. So important is this quality that, at certain levels, it trumps every other quality for succeeding at work. It doesn't matter if you are hardworking and your team members like you; if C-suite perceives that you are not loyal, your career will be stunted. People you are better than, in your assessment, will be promoted above you and given more senior and sensitive responsibilities.

I once worked with two senior managers who were both on the same grade. However, when it was time for the appointment to the executive management position, one was bypassed, and the other made an executive director. The main reason wasn't performance-related because both were doing great in their respective divisions. The main reason was the loyalty to the Chairman of the organisation.

Someone might complain that it is not fair. Let me ask you: if you have two strong people in terms of performance and you want to appoint only one of them, which other dimension would you look out for?

More than ever, employers are looking for people who will be loyal to them, to their mission and purpose, and who will be there for the long haul. The higher you want to climb, the more critical it is for you to be in the good books of those up there.

To understand loyalty, we need to differentiate it from trust, politics, sycophancy, and blind followership.

Loyalty and Trust

Although they are similar, they are not the same. Trust or trustworthiness deals with the reliability of someone's character or competence. Can I predict that the person will do what they said they would do? That's trust. When we trust people, we know that they will do what they say they will do. For example, I trust my staff to show up on time and do a good job.

However, loyalty goes beyond what you do to where your heart is. It is about motive and allegiance to someone or their cause. Am I safe with you? Can I guarantee that you will always act in my best interest? Look at it this way. Josephine can be trusted to do a good job—her numbers are good, but the board members questioned her allegiance—where her heart is. Is it to herself or to the organisation? That's the difference.

"So important is loyalty that, at certain levels, it trumps every other quality for succeeding at work."

Perhaps to understand the difference between loyalty and trust, we need to look at the opposite meaning of both words. The opposite of trust is distrust, while the opposite of loyalty is disloyalty or betrayal. An untrustworthy person will miss targets, appointments, and deadlines; a disloyal person will sell us out and stab us behind the back. With an untrustworthy person, you have broken promises with heartaches; with a disloyal person, you have heartbreaks!

Loyalty and Politics

Loyalty and politics are not the same. As we have explained, loyalty is a heart allegiance to a person or cause, while politics is about personal interests.

Organisations can be broadly divided into two based on their leanings to either the political or performance dimensions. In some organisations, politics is the order of the day, and performance goes out of the window. In such organisations, mediocres are promoted based on their political networks. Such organisations and nations are doomed to fail. Some other organisations lean towards the performance dimension, and performance is celebrated and rewarded. However, there are no purely performance-driven organisations. The higher you climb the organisational ladder, the more critical the political dimension becomes.

Every organisation, no matter how performance-focused, has an element of politics. What is politics? It is simply the alignment of interests in order to achieve a favourable outcome within the organisation. That favourable outcome might be getting a good posting, promotion, or career opportunities. It is ensuring that you are in the good books of the key decision-makers that you achieve favourable decisions.

You can see that politics is not bad. It is aligning with key influencers to make work easier for you. It is not the dirty politics of putting others down. As they say in international politics, "There are no permanent friends or permanent enemies; only permanent interests." The higher you want to climb, the more important it is for you to understand your organisational politics and use it to your advantage.

Someone recently shared a story with me. She is recognised for her performance every year but bypassed when it comes to promotions, and others are promoted ahead of her. The reason? She doesn't play politics, as she puts it. But she has learnt her lesson. And she teaches her team members to understand organisational politics and use it to their advantage. It is wisdom to understand your organisational politics and use it to your advantage. But please separate politics from loyalty. There are many "politicians" who are not loyal. They are sycophants! Most politicians cannot subordinate their personal interests for the good of their nations or organisations.

Loyalty, Sycophancy and Blind Followership

Some people confuse loyalty with sycophancy and blind followership. Therefore, we need to differentiate the three concepts to avoid such confusion.

A sycophant has a selfish and ulterior motive. They praise and act favourably towards you because of what they stand to gain. They do not have your interest at heart. When they see the truth, they colour it if it will affect either their position with you or what they stand to gain from you. They tell you what you want to hear and not what you need to hear. The day you leave or are removed, their "loyalty" shifts immediately to the next person in power or authority for their personal benefit.

A blind follower, on the other hand, follows without thinking. They don't do independent thinking. If you ask them to do something unethical, they will do it without asking questions. Whereas a sycophant knows it is unethical but will not say so, a blind follower doesn't know and doesn't care. Their attitude is, "The boss said I should do it, and so be it." They live by the "order from above" mindset. To them, they feel exonerated since they are following orders. They simply did what they were told to do.

Finally, a loyal staff acts favourably not because of what they stand to gain but because it is right. If a decision is wrong, they will speak up and challenge you with respect out of their love for you and their passion for the organisation. One of my associates once said to me, "My loyalty to you means I have to tell you the truth. What you do with it is your business." That's what real loyalty is—to care for someone or something so much that you are willing to risk your standing with that person to be objective and truthful with them.

Three Levels of Loyalty

Now that we know what real loyalty is, we need to consider the three levels of loyalty for an employee—organisation, team, and individual. As you can see from the diagram below, your highest level of loyalty should be to your organisation (after God, of course!).

Organisational Loyalty

The oganisation is the glue that binds us together. Without the organisation, we would not have the relationships we have at work or even a job in the first place. Therefore, the first filter in decision-making should be: is this in the best interest of my organisation? Or how would this help to further the cause of my organisation?

Organisations are looking for loyal employees because they will act in their best interest. They can also be trusted with critical and sensitive organisational assignments.

Below are some action plans to help you get started on building organisational loyalty:

Do A Good Job

I believe loyalty begins with a commitment to excellence. You were employed to do a job; your loyalty is to ensure you do a great job. The willingness to go the extra mile to deliver excellence is the starting point of loyalty. Sychophants and praise singers are not concerned about the quality of their jobs.

Love Your Company

Another quality of loyal employees is that they are proud to be associated with their organisations. Love is often a matter of focus. Loyal employees choose to focus on the good things about their organisations. Using the Pareto principle, the 80:20 rule, the best companies are only eighty per cent great. The challenge with most people is where they choose to put their focus. Loyal employees choose to focus on the good things about their company—the eighty per cent. They do not deny the twenty per cent weakness, but they choose to focus on the good eighty per cent.

Many years ago, I heard the story of an employee who went to her executive coach and told him she wanted to resign from her company. Below is my recollection of the story.

"Why?" asked the executive coach. "Because I hate my job!" replied the employee.

"Why do you hate your job?" asked the coach. And the woman listed a catalogue of the things she hated about the job and her company.

The executive coach then asked her if there was anything good about her job or company? She categorically said no. (Sometimes, when we are so focused on the negatives, we do not see the positives).

The executive coach prodded further and asked, "Do they pay your salaries regularly and on time?" She answered in the affirmative. "That's one good thing about your company," the coach replied.

"Do you enjoy what you do?" She answered yes.

"Do you have great friends at work?" he queried. "Of course. My work colleagues are amazing."

They worked together until they arrived at a good list of the positive things about her job and company. He then challenged her to focus on the good things about her job and company for the next thirty days and report back. And if she was still willing to resign after thirty days, he would encourage her to do so.

After thirty days, he saw a different woman. She was full of life and energy. She said, "I am not resigning again. I never knew I had a lot going on for me that I was about to throw away because of a temporary challenge at work."

That's what the power of focus does. Loyal employees do not deny their company's bad or challenging aspects; they simply choose to focus on the good parts. (Sometimes, however, we may have to leave, and we will deal more with this later).

Respect Boundaries

Loyalty to your organisation is also seen in respecting the company's boundaries. Certain behaviours are seen as anathema by the organisation. Avoid them. For Adam, it was simple: avoid the tree of knowledge of good and evil *"...for in the day that you eat of it you shall surely die."*

What, for you, is like the tree of the knowledge of good and evil that if you eat, will result in "death?" Avoid them like a plague.

Boundaries can be divided into three: policies, values, and landmines.

Policies are the non-negotiable instructions that you must not violate. They are usually communicated during onboarding. They are like the ten commandments of work:
- Thou shall not have any other business outside this business. (Some organisations allow their staff to run other businesses as long as it does not conflict with the business of the organisation).
- Thou shall not defraud a customer or conspire with a customer or colleague to defraud the organisation.
- Thou shall not divulge our trade secrets.
- Thou shall not sexually harass thy colleague.

To remain in an organisation, you must adhere to the policy boundaries.

Values are usually behaviour-related boundaries seen in your company's organisational core values. Here, loyalty is being an ambassador of your organisational values. Live them!

Landmines are people you must avoid or tread carefully with. They fall into two categories:
- *Power brokers*: In every system, there are key influencers. They go by different names—the "cabal" or "management children". There is wisdom in recognising such people. It has nothing to do with their level in the organisation. For example, a middle manager can exert more influence in a system than even an executive. Your duty is to find such people and tread carefully with them. Do not go out of your way to challenge them unless they too have crossed the line and want you to do something unethical. Make it your goal to have at least one key influencer as your advocate. It will make work easier for you.

- *Those in management's bad books.* One of my former bosses advised me not to associate with someone who has been "marked for death." If someone is ostracised due to boundaries they have crossed, and management is bidding time to terminate their appointment, you need to tread carefully with such people. Associating with them might breed suspicion and cast you in a bad light too. Be diplomatic in your relationship with them. You might become guilty by association.

Ask Tough Questions

Loyal employees are not "yes" people. Instead, because they care enough about the company's success, they will ask tough decisions about the company's direction, strategy, and investment decisions. And they are not afraid to inform management when such decisions would backfire, although they do so with respect.

I once had a staff member who, whenever I called for a meeting and presented my idea, would say to me that my idea was fantastic. At first, I thought my idea was awesome. But I noticed that it was his pattern. "Great. Fantastic. Nice. I am okay with it." Finally, I got so frustrated and told him, "Please stop. If I thought my idea was fantastic, there would be no reason for me to bring it out in the open for debate. I am looking for how to improve the idea." Sycophancy sucks!

Guess what? I also noticed another member who would challenge my ideas, sometimes to the point of telling me that they would not work. And every time I overrode him, I noticed that the idea would backfire just as he said. What did I do? He became my closest confidant. I would never make a major decision without his opinion. Those are the kind of staff organisations are looking for—those who will respect authority but also be truthful to authority.

Defend Institutional Integrity
Although they ask tough questions in private and sometimes disagree with management or the organisation's decision, they do not go about telling others how stupid the decision is. As long as such decisions are not unethical or do not infringe on people's fundamental human rights, once they are made, they abide by them and speak up for their management in public. They do not speak against their institutions in public or stab their bosses behind their backs. Many years ago, I wrote an article on what I call *The Marriage Creed*. And one of the points I wrote there was *Agree to Disagree*. I said that when two people always agree, one person is playing the role of a fool. There will be disagreements. We will not come to a common understanding on all issues. But maturity is knowing how to manage our disputes. The immature will throw a tantrum and tell the entire world about their disagreement. The mature will respect the authority of their superiors and follow on with the idea as long as it is not unethical. And even if the idea goes bad, they don't go about telling the whole world, "I told you so." Josephine needs to learn this point. She is known to speak up in public against some of management's decisions.

Attend Company's Events
To succeed in today's world of work, you need to blend in, to become "one of them" without losing your individuality or identity. Lone rangers might be heroes in movies, but in real life, they are villains. People misinterpret their lone ranger attitude as pride or as someone difficult to get along with.

There are so many ways to blend in, but one important way is to attend company events. As simple as this is, it is also another way leaders measure loyalty to the company. If you consistently miss your company's organised events and do not make out time to socialize and get to meet the senior partners of your organisation, you are robbing yourself of the opportunity to network and build your brand. In today's world of work, it is not only what you know and can bring to the table that counts; who you know is as important, if not more important, than what you know. Herein lies another of Josephine's problems. She was not visible to the board members. As a senior member of the management team, she doesn't attend social events because, in her opinion, they are just a waste of her time. And she doesn't hide her feelings about such events from the other divisional heads.

In blending in, please don't lose your individuality. Be authentic. Don't compromise your values in order to blend in. Should you attend a strip club because you want to blend in? I don't think so. You can get the team to change the venue for the social gathering from a strip club to a regular club.

Don't Hold Your Organisation to Ransom
Nobody likes being a hostage—whether as an individual or a company. Sometimes, people hold their organisations to ransom by forcing them to match offers. They negotiate with an organisation with no intention of taking the offer but use it to negotiate with their current organisation to get a higher salary. As a friend told me, everybody loses in the end. The first organisation gave you the offer in good faith; by using it as a basis of negotiation and not taking up the offer, you break a bond of loyalty with them. You might have scored a win because your organisation renegotiated your salary, but you leave a bad taste in your organisation and send a message that you are not a loyal staff. At the end of the day, everyone loses somehow.

What would I recommend? Never start a job search until you are ready to leave. And when you are offered a job that meets your demands, don't look back except in rare situations. Now, if your current organisation asks you to reconsider your resignation and, of their own volition, agrees to match the offer, then you may have to think about that. But do not take their offer and go back to the new organisation and ask them to make you a counteroffer. You do not want to be known as a Judas before you start. Whatever you decide eventually, please ensure that you do not force or arm-twist people into making you an offer just like Josephine did to her organisation.

Also, if you must leave, do not leave with immediate effect. This is particularly important at senior levels. Give your current organisation the compulsory notice period so that they can prepare someone else to take over your role. Do not burn the bridge you have built for five, ten, or even twenty years because of a new job offer. How you leave will determine whether you can come back to the same organisation in the future.

> *"Blend in but don't lose your individuality."*

The Limits of Organisational Loyalty

Now a caveat. While loyalty is an important quality, remember that you should be loyal to your organisation as long as they do not violate your moral codes. Suppose your organisation wants you to do something unethical, to violate universal principles that you hold dear, one that defines who you are. What should you do?

In that case, you need to redefine what loyalty means. Loyalty is not the same as blind followership, as we have noted earlier. If, for example, your organisation wants you to steal trade secrets, commit adultery to get an account from a customer, or lie against someone so that they can sack that person. They, too, have crossed the line. Just as organisations have boundaries, you too should have your own boundaries that your organisation should not cross. And you cannot be loyal to such an extent that you violate your moral codes. You will be accountable before God and man. The thousands who lost their jobs, and some their lives, in the Arthur Andersen and Enron's scandal is a silent reminder that we should be loyal to our organisations only so far as they too do not violate known universal principles. So please do not go to jail for any organisation. It is just not worth it!

> *"Lone rangers might be heroes in movies, but in real life, they are villains. People misinterpret their lone ranger attitude as pride or as someone difficult to get along with."*

Team and Individual Loyalty

The next level of loyalty is loyalty to your team, including your boss (we will consider simple strategies for managing your boss in the next chapter). But loyalty to your team should be subservient to your allegiance to the organisation. When we put team loyalty ahead of organisational loyalty, the end result is division, silo mentality, and turf wars. Yes, be loyal to your team but not to the detriment of the organisation.

The final level of loyalty is loyalty to the individual members of the team. However, this should not affect your dedication and commitment to the team. Don't be so loyal to an individual member at the team's expense. Don't celebrate an individual to the extent that you create acrimony among the other team members. You must be seen to be fair to all in the team.

Consider the following case of misplaced loyalty to an individual member. I once heard the story of a head of human resources in a bank that had an affair with a staff member.

During the promotions of staff, the promotion committee sat and made their recommendations. Unfortunately, his lady friend did not make it. Assuming that the committee members would not know, he secretly inserted the lady's name in the list and released the list. His thought was: "What could possibly go wrong? They would never find out. She is just one person among the hundreds promoted." However, someone in the promotion committee noticed a disparity between the number promoted and the number recommended for promotion and requested for the original list. Having discovered the anomaly, he raised a query to the management, and the head of HR lost his job.

This is a classic case of misplaced loyalty. He was more loyal to the individual than he was to the organisation. Sometimes people have misplaced loyalty too. They fight and defend their people to the extent that they put themselves against the organisation. The organisation brought us together. Without the organisation, we would never have known each other. Therefore, our first loyalty should be to the organisation, before the team we belong to (our departments and units), and finally, to the people we work with (the individuals).

Should I be loyal when I feel that the organisation is not where I should be or want to be?

Stella attended a seminar where the concept of loyalty to the organisation was taught. While she liked the concept, she feels it is not applicable to her situation. This is not her dream job. In fact, she is ashamed to tell people that she is working for a small and relatively unknown company. Right now, she is just waiting for a big break. When she finds the company of her dreams, then the concept of loyalty would be relevant but not before. What advice would you give her?

There are many people in Stella's position. Sometimes we do not get exactly what we want, but like a game of cards, we are supposed to make the best of the cards life has given to us. We, like Stella, have two options: to be loyal even though the organisation is not our dream job or to wait until we get our dream job before we start being loyal.

There are two challenges with waiting before being committed or loyal:

- We may never get the dream breaks we want as life sees us as unworthy of them. Too often, many people do not live their lives because they are waiting for their big breaks. Their life becomes like a game that was never played, a book that was never written, and a song that was never composed. By waiting, they missed the opportunity to live.
- Even when we get our dream breaks, we will destroy such opportunities because we have not learned what loyalty is.

Many people dream of greatness. They see themselves as billionaires, CEOs of multinational corporations, or retiring early and settling down in a remote Fijian island. But they forget that the rite of passage into their great dreams is through work. And, sometimes, life will test us with small opportunities and positions to see whether we are ready for the big breaks. Those who cannot work where they find themselves and demonstrate loyalty where they are might never get to where they want to be in life.

I believe destiny is a collection of experiences and relationships. Therefore, every experience, even our mistakes and misadventures, is part of the process of shaping us for destiny.

Destiny doesn't happen in one fell swoop; it is not a straight line but one with detours and contours. Yet, as painful as they may be, the detours and contours are necessary to shape us and prepare us for our ultimate destiny.

But the key that will unlock your destiny is being loyal irrespective of where you find yourself and discharging your responsibility with excellence. Therefore, Stella, while this might not be your dream job, you need to learn and demonstrate loyalty right where you are. If you cannot learn loyalty right now in your small organisation, you will not be loyal in a big organisation. The truth is, you may never get your big breaks if you do not start now to demonstrate loyalty.

See your small job as a training ground, a launchpad for the great future life has in store for you. Small beginnings do not mean small destinies.

Should I be loyal when I feel the organisation has not been fair to me?

What if you have given your best to the organisation and the organisation has taken advantage of you? For example, promises have not been kept, and you have missed several promotions. What should you do? Should you still be loyal?

Loyalty is a two-way street. Many years ago, I attended a seminar where someone taught loyalty more from blind followership. Although the CEO was very pleased, the message left a bad taste and did not achieve the desired effect. Just as organisations demand loyalty, so should they also be loyal to their employees. If you find yourself in an organisation that demands loyalty but is not loyal to its people, the best option is to quit and look for another organisation that will value your services. (See when you should leave below).

While this option is the best, we know that it is not readily available for many people. With job scarcity, we may have to explore other options. Also, there is no guarantee that you will not experience the same thing in your new place.

What, then, is the next best option? I believe it is to make the best of your current situation while hoping for a breakthrough. Although not a very easy option, it is the next best option. What is the least effective option? Remain and undermine your organisation: complain, bicker, and tell the world how your organisation has been unfair to you.

I recently saw a video of a newscaster who complained about not being paid during a live broadcast. Having read the initial headline news, he digressed and announced that they were being owed their salaries for some months. While he may get his salary and the arrears, he has potentially blocked the opportunity to get another job. Which employer would want someone to broadcast their inability to pay salaries to the world?

The problem with complaining is that it makes the situation worse. Studies in brain sciences have shown that complaining changes you for the worse. It makes the brain more attuned to notice other negative events in your life. It wires the brain to recognise negative events. People who complain about events at work are more likely to see more negative events at home, on the road, in their relationships. Thus, complaining changes you into a negative person, and by the law of attraction, you emit negative energy and attract negative events into your life. So, it is worth it? No.

Stop complaining. Your organisation might not be perfect. The nature of your job might not be perfect. You might have a difficult boss. Rather than complain, work hard, and commit your case to God, trusting Him to open the door to the next phase of your destiny for you. Whilst there, look for the opportunity to address the issues instead of broadcasting them to the world.

When to Leave

There comes a time when you may have to leave the organisation. Knowing when to leave is very important. Beyond the issue of relocating or going back to school to further your education, here are my top seven reasons to leave an organisation:

- *You are not growing.* The first reason to consider leaving a job is a lack of personal growth. One of the benefits of working is the opportunity to grow and develop. If you are stuck and are not growing, then it is time to think about a job change. In Maslow's hierarchy of needs is the concept of self-actualisation. Self-actualisation is impossible if the job doesn't provide you with challenges and opportunities to learn new things.
- *You have found a new job.* Hopefully, this new job aligns with your career interests, provides you with the opportunity to learn and grow, and has a great culture.
- *Your current company is undergoing a major crisis or an acquisition.* Sometimes, you need to read the handwriting on the wall. A major crisis, a new buyer, or the company is undergoing a merger and acquisition are indications to start thinking of a job change.
- *There are conflicts in values—the organisation wants you to compromise on your boundaries.* We have talked about personal boundaries earlier. Never cross your personal boundaries for an organisation.
- *It is affecting something valuable like your health or family.* Sometimes, the company isn't bad, but the workload and

scheduling hours are putting a strain on some important aspects of your life, like your health and family. You may need to negotiate with the company to help you balance the competing demands of work with the other aspects of your life. If they cannot, you may want to look for another job, even if it is with a pay cut.

- *Your life is in danger.* My younger brother once had an offer for an IT job in Afghanistan in 2020. He asked for my opinion, and I told him not to bother. The difference in salary is not worth his life. From the benefit of hindsight, we are grateful he didn't take the job with the Taliban now in charge of Afghanistan.
- *The tug of destiny.* Sometimes, you know within your gut that it is time to leave. There is nothing wrong with the organisation, but the tug of destiny within you is calling you to strike out a new career path, whatever that path may be. Once you are certain, you need to follow your gut instincts and move on even if you do not have all the answers. For example, Elon Musk was a PhD student at Stanford. He left after two days to pursue his entrepreneurial dreams. Sometimes, the work environment is not the problem. Destiny has something greater in store for you.

Whatever be thy reason for leaving, please do not leave with a bitter heart and do not burn thy bridges. If you do these two, you will be fine.

CHAPTER EIGHT

MANAGE WELL THY BOSS

Uchenna is very angry with his boss, Ronke. According to him, she is everything not to like in a boss. Unlike his former boss, Bisi, who was easygoing, friendly, and empathetic, this new boss (only God knows where they employed her from) is too direct, rigid, and impersonal. Gone were the usual office banter and the TGIFs. Now it is work, work, and more work. While Bisi would overlook some of their mistakes and correct them herself, Ronke would insist they fix the errors themselves and correct them again and again until they get it right. Uchenna is exasperated. He wished he could press a fairy-tale reset button and go back to how things were before Ronke came. Not only is Uchenna angry with Ronke, but he is also surprised that some of his colleagues have moved on. Once, while complaining about Ronke, Aminu, one of his colleagues, told him, "Ronke isn't that bad; you just need to get to know her, and you would like her." "God forbid!" Uchenna screamed. "There is nothing to like about her." Use the lessons in this chapter to help Uchenna manage his boss.

MANAGE WELL THY BOSS

One of the most important relationships to manage in the workplace is the relationship with your boss. Many people have destroyed a promising career because they couldn't manage their bosses.

The truth is, managing people is a messy and challenging business. Those of us who have kids know how difficult it is to manage them! Even with all the authority and the threat of sanctions, it is still not easy managing them. With your boss, there is an inverse power relationship. She has all the "power", so you cannot use threats and sanctions against her. And guess what? She has her idiosyncrasies, weaknesses, and nuisance value. But if you must succeed in the workplace, you must learn to manage her with all her baggage.

In this chapter, we will look at universal principles of managing bosses. Of course, bosses are different, as Uchenna discovered. And while there is not a one-size-fits-all approach to managing bosses, there are certain commonalities across the different types of bosses that will help you manage your boss very well.

Why Manage Your Boss?

You may be wondering why you need to manage your boss. You have your own challenges, so why add the challenge of managing someone else, especially your boss?

There are several reasons why you need to manage your boss, but I will consider only three:

- *To make work easier for you.* Managing your boss makes life and work easier for you. Your boss is the gateway between you and the next line of authority. Since most of your work will go through your boss, it pays you to have a good working relationship with her. If not, she might become an obstacle, and your work might never get noticed.
- *To advance your career.* Your boss can also create opportunities including but not limited to training and higher responsibilities that will help position you for more significant roles in the organisation. Also, it pays to have your boss as an ally. Making your boss your adversary is one way to destroy your career, especially if your boss is well connected within the organisation or industry. If you do not have a good working relationship with your boss, you will find out that sometimes it doesn't matter how good you are, someone else might be promoted over you. Imagine a scenario where a boss was leaving and was asked who would replace her, and she bypassed her direct report and chose the person below her direct report for the job.
- *For your peace of mind.* One of the most important reasons for managing your boss is for your own peace of mind. Do you want to go home every day complaining about your hostile work environment, or do you want to look forward to going to work? A critical part of job fulfilment is the quality of the relationship you have with your boss. And if you have a poor working relationship with your boss, it will affect your state of mind and health. So, if your sanity means anything to you, you need to invest time to develop a good working relationship with your boss.

How to Manage Your Boss

There are so many books about managing bosses, but there are broadly only two ways to manage your boss: based on the task dimension of working and the relational dimension. The goal of the task dimension is to ensure that you meet your expectations and deliver excellence on the job, while the goal of the relational dimension is to ensure that you have a good working relationship with her. Do these two, and you would have no problem with managing your boss or any other boss.

Let's consider specific strategies under each dimension.

Managing Your Boss—Task Dimension

Play Well Thy Role

Managing your boss is like acting in a movie. You only need to know two things: the script and the expectations of the director. And then act accordingly.

The first thing in managing your boss is whatever your script, act well thy part. Whatever expectations the organisation has given you, meet and exceed them.

You were employed to do a job—just do it! One of the most fundamental issues with managing one's boss is performance-related: not meeting a deadline, missed targets, or report errors. Other issues deal with personality and style-related issues or the relational dimension.

Remember our four-part component of work? Output, standard, satisfaction, and reward. Every output elicits an emotional reaction from our bosses, as we have said earlier. Whenever you do a poor job, your boss will be dissatisfied, and that dissatisfaction might cause her to speak to you angrily. However, if you deliver excellence with the right attitude, you most likely will not have problems managing your boss. Instead, your boss will be delighted with your work, and it will lead to a good working relationship with her.

Clarify Specific Expectations
Doing your job well is the starting point. Sometimes, however, your boss might give you a specific job to do. What should you do? Clarify her expectations. While doing your job is more of speed and execution, clarifying expectations is largely getting the right direction at the outset. You sure do not want to move fast in the wrong direction!

A key principle to learn here is this: never leave the place of assignment without knowing the what, when and how. Better to ask now and clarify expectations than to look stupid later.

Help Your Boss to Succeed
Who is a boss? Someone that is ultimately responsible for the performance of the team. The boss is the one who has the primary assignment. Irrespective of your job title, as long as you work in a unit and have a reporting line, your role is to help your boss look good. Therefore, do the following:

- *Never compete with your boss for relevance.* Even if you are technically more proficient than your boss, do not compete with your boss for relevance. You are here to help and not to compete with her. Even if she takes your ideas and shines with them, be grateful that she found them helpful enough to use. Don't go about telling others that it was your idea or your report. Undermining your boss will not further your career.
- *Take on added responsibility for your boss.* Sometimes, just by asking your boss if there is any work assignment she wants someone to do and volunteering to help will go a long way. Every boss likes the staff who will go the extra

mile for them. Let her know she can always count on you. However, it will be impossible to do this if you have not consistently delivered excellence on your job.
- *Help the team to succeed.* Your boss is responsible for the performance of the team and not just individual members. So, if you can help the team to succeed or help colleagues when necessary, you are also helping your boss.
- *Align with your boss's vision and speak your boss's language.* Be the staff that the boss knows is on her side. This is not flattery or political correctness. She is the boss. The vision is hers. Support it and champion it. If you think the vision needs tweaking, then arrange a meeting to discuss it over. But by all means, support her vision.

Consider the following true-life example. James (not his real name) was a contract staff in a bank. He was the laughing stock of his colleagues because his boss used to give him extra work. They called him madam's dumping ground. While others were idling away or would leave for the day, James would stay behind to finish the boss's extra work assigned to him. One day, he went for an interview in another bank. After the initial preambles, they asked him to describe his normal day-to-day duties. When James finished describing the tasks he accomplishes daily, the interviewers were stunned. They informed him that what he just described is the responsibility of staff three levels above him in their bank. He was offered the job on the spot. The people who laughed at him couldn't laugh any longer. Looking back, James attributed his change in fortunes to his boss, who gave him responsibilities beyond his level and pushed him beyond his comfort zone.

Managing Your Boss—Relational Dimension

Know Well Your Boss

People are different! As obvious as this truth is, many people do not accept the fact that people are different. They want others to think and act like them. They struggle with people's differences and complain when those differences deviate from their definition of "normal" behaviour, and, usually, that definition is from their perspectives. Some of us, like Uchenna, wish we could mould our bosses to fit our view of life. We discover, sometimes too late, that we cannot mould or change our bosses; we must accept them for who they are and work with them. Curiously, when we accept them for who they are, we find it easier to influence them to change for the better. But not before. Acceptance must come first before influence.

To accept your boss, you must know her—her strengths and weaknesses. The ancient Greeks have an aphorism, "Know thyself." This admonition also applies to managing your boss: "Know thy boss."

Working effectively with your boss requires you to know who your boss is. And knowing your boss begins by understanding her predictable patterns of behaviours or dominant traits.

Why is it important to understand your boss's dominant traits? Because people will always be true to their dominant characteristics. Their modes of working, preferences, and reactions to issues flow from their dominant personality traits. Bisi, Uchenna's former boss, is easygoing, friendly, and empathetic, while Ronke, his new boss, is direct, rigid, and impersonal. These predictable patterns of behaviours are called personality traits or temperaments from the Greek philosopher Galen, who modified Hippocrates four body fluids into the concept of temperaments. He coined the commonly used words to describe people's temperaments: sanguine, melancholic, choleric, and phlegmatic.

Today, there are different models to identify people's dominant characteristics which are beyond the scope of this chapter. However, irrespective of which model you are familiar with, please consider what I call the five essentials to know about your boss:
- *Perspectives*: How does she see things?
- *Priorities*: What is important to her?
- *Preferences*: How does she want things done?
- *Pursuits*: What motivates and drives her?
- *Problems*: What triggers her and her response to them?

Knowing these five things would help you better manage your boss.

DIFFERENT TYPES OF BOSSES

Beyond the personality classification, here are some types of bosses you will meet in the workplace:

Perfectionist. Wants things done in a certain way. Great attention to detail. Quality trumps speed. Sometimes late in producing a report because she wants the report to be perfect. Rigid and inflexible.

Narcissist. Thinks the whole world revolves around her. Overinflated ego. Likes the spotlight. Wants to be in control. Manipulative. Never accepts responsibility for her mistakes. Always plays the blame game and victimhood.

Driver. Results-oriented. No excuses. Pushes people to achieve stretch targets. Will provide some coaching and support and will celebrate you and reward you for achieving the result.

Slavemaster. Like the driver, this boss will push you to achieve results, but unlike the driver, she will not provide any support or coaching and take all the glory herself. Aggressive.

Friendly. Easygoing boss. Focus is more on the emotional wellbeing of her team. Team is like a great social club. Cannot hold people accountable for performance. Talks too much and lacks follow-through.

Clueless. Does not know that she does not know. Has been promoted beyond her level of competence and has no desire to learn and grow. Subordinates are left to figure things out themselves.

Evil Genius. Diabolical and unethical. Untrustworthy. Will lead you down the road to hell and disown you. Always looking for a way to beat the system.

Insecure. Afraid of team members outshining them. Immobilised by the fear of failure. Attention seeker. Surrounds self with sycophants. Sees good subordinates as threats.

Adapt Your Style

You have one boss, and it is not the boss's responsibility to adjust her style to fit yours; it is your responsibility to adapt and fit into her working style. Why do I say so? Your boss might have two or twenty-two direct reports. You don't expect her to adjust to twenty-two different individuals. The responsibility of her direct reports is to understudy her and adapt their styles to hers.

I once worked with a boss who was outgoing, loud, and friendly. I approached him with my direct, business-oriented, and sense of urgency traits. It didn't give me the results I wanted. But the day I switched my style and related with him from his style, my working relationship with him improved. And so also my results.

Just like Aminu advised Uchenna to get to know his new boss and adjust his approach, you also need to know your boss and change your approach.

Respect Your Boss

Everybody wants to feel important. People's behaviours reinforce, protect, or defend their feeling of importance. When people respect us, they make us feel important, and we gravitate towards them. They earn the right to enter our inner world because their respect for us has given them access to our inner chamber.

But when they disrespect us, the natural human tendency is to protect our feeling of importance. So we become defensive and attack them, like a bulldog trying to fight off an intruder.

Most times, the reaction we get from our bosses is largely determined by their perception of our respect towards them. Notice I said the perception of our respect. If your boss doesn't feel you respect her, don't be surprised when your requests are delayed or rejected. And at the slightest opportunity, don't be surprised at your boss's exaggerated response towards you like a bulldog. Our bosses' aggression stems from either a personality weakness or the fight response to a perceived threat. So, just before you blame her aggressiveness on a personality weakness, ask yourself whether you are contributing to it.

Never forget that your boss's response to you is determined primarily by her perception of your respect for her. Your respect for her validates her feeling of importance. By making her feel important, she will do everything to protect the relationship she has with you.

So, can you show respect to your boss?

Here are some ways to show respect to your boss:

- *Respect her authority.* You need not like all her decisions. But because she is the boss, you need to respect her decisions.
- *Never take privileges for granted.* Some people have friendly and empathetic bosses, and instead of respecting them, they begin to take them for granted. Because the boss is understanding, they start showing up late, making excuses to take a day off, or submitting reports late. Then when the boss cuts off those privileges, they turn and accuse their

boss of being mean. Never take privileges for granted. Having a nice boss is a privilege. Please don't abuse it.
- *Communicate often with her.* No boss likes to be surprised by hearing information about the team or ongoing tasks from those outside her team. Do not let her hear critical information about the team or ongoing tasks from outsiders. Keep her in the loop about critical projects.
- *Never undermine your boss behind her back.* Of course, if you disagree with a position, find a suitable time to address it with your boss. However, do not start a campaign of calumny against your boss.
- *Focus on her strengths.* Your boss is not perfect. Most bosses have obvious weaknesses. The challenge with many staff members is that instead of focusing on the boss's strengths, they focus on her weaknesses. What they forget is that whatever they focus on magnifies. If you focus on the boss's weaknesses, that's the only thing you will see. Therefore, learn to celebrate her strengths and manage her weaknesses. Don't go gossiping about her weakness.
- *Be loyal.* We have covered loyalty in the previous chapter.

Apply Emotional Intelligence

Your boss is both a rational and an emotional being. As an emotional being, your boss has moods. Success in managing your boss is catching her in the right mood.

Today, many bosses are under pressure to deliver business results. And pressure causes people to react or easily lose their temper. You can choose to focus on her reaction and judge her, or you can choose to understand the cause of her reaction and empathise with her.

What would emotional and social intelligence do for you? Staff with a high sense of social awareness can pick up emotional cues in their boss's tone of voice and behaviours. They easily distinguish between primary (standard behaviours) from secondary behaviours (behaviours under pressure and emotional tension). They know when the boss is under pressure and in a bad mood. And what do they do?

- First, they show empathy by not judging their boss's moods and secondary behaviours.
- Second, they ensure they don't add to the boss's pressure by managing social distance and doing a good job.
- Third, they engage their bosses to try and diffuse the tension through empathetic listening.

Change Your Perspective
Closely related to the above concept is changing your perspective and seeing your boss's weaknesses in a new light. How we think about a situation is often the root cause of our emotional problems and tension. By looking at a situation differently, we can reduce the emotional intensity of that situation.

One of the quickest ways to diffuse emotional stress is to change our perspectives about issues. We now know that our emotions follow the direction of our focus and the meaning and interpretation we give to events. Changing our focus or how we interpret things will change our emotional experience about that issue.

Let me share with you a personal example to illustrate this concept. Many years ago, I found myself in an organisation that I wondered how I got there. The boss had some obvious leadership flaws. Every day I said to myself that I made a terrible mistake joining the organisation and regretted my decision. And every day, my anger and resentment increased. Every mistake of my boss became magnified before me and gave me another reason to complain. Then, one day, as I asked myself, "How did I get here?" I heard the following words: "Perhaps God brought you here to learn how not to lead." That was an epiphany for me. It was such a transformative moment. Suddenly, the leader's weaknesses became a blessing in disguise and a rich source of leadership insights, some of which have made me the person I am today. Gone was my anger about his weaknesses. Instead, my focus or perspective was now on the lessons I could learn from his weaknesses.

Imagine if you take the same principle and apply it to your current situation. You see, there are two ways we learn: through wisdom, and from experience. Wisdom is learning and doing the right thing at the right time, the first time. Experience is learning from your mistakes. Sometimes, it takes experience to know wisdom.

See your demanding boss as an experiential wisdom lesson in leadership. Take everything negative and turn them into positive lessons. For example, if your boss is aggressive, the wisdom lesson is that you should develop patience and self-control. You do not need someone to teach you about self-control and patience. He is the best teacher you can have because you know first-hand the importance and impact of a lack of self-control. If your boss is an evil genius, the lesson is integrity. If your boss is clueless, the lesson is expert knowledge and being on top of the game. You get the idea.

When you do not turn such experiences into wisdom lessons, not only will you keep experiencing the emotional tension of their behaviours, but you also condemn yourself to repeating the same mistakes. This is the reason people become the replica of the bosses they once loathed. But once you change your perspectives about your boss's weaknesses, you will no longer be immobilised by them. Instead, their shortcomings become empowering lessons for you as you journey through life.

So, what should Uchenna do? See Ronke's insistence on him correcting his mistakes as an opportunity to improve his attention to detail and her business-like focus as helping him improve his work ethic.

Sometimes, difficult bosses are life's way of preparing us for greater opportunities ahead.

Reciprocal Influence

This final piece is like a summary of the whole concept of managing your boss. You see, influence is reciprocal. Your boss has formal authority over you and most times uses this authority to get things done. You obey, not because you want to, but because you have to. But as we noted earlier, you do not have any formal authority over your boss. Your only means of influencing her is your informal power or authority.

Below is my simple triangle of influence.

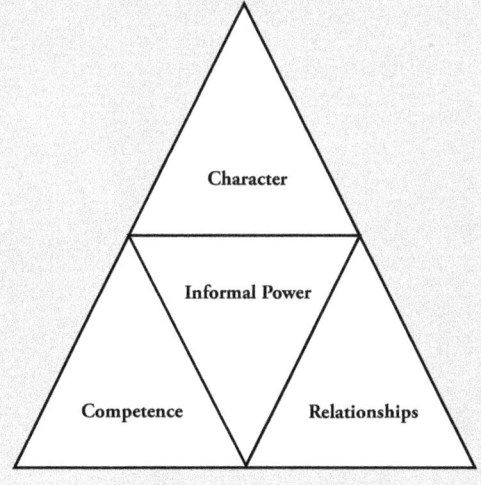

Triangle of informal power

There are three major things you need to develop to have informal power and influence with your boss, and they are:

- *Character:* be known as a person of character and integrity. Be trustworthy. Honour your word and keep your promises. Be professional in your relationships with colleagues and customers.
- *Competence:* be an authority in your area. Deliver excellence on your job. Provide unique solutions to organisational problems.
- *Relationships:* develop a good relationship with your boss. Invest the time necessary to develop a working relationship with your boss. Demonstrate the attitude of loyalty.

Do these three, and you will find that even the most difficult bosses can become great friends!

APPENDIX

APPENDIX A

THE PROPORTION OF WORK AND WORK-RELATED HOURS

Number of hours in a week	**168 hours**
Average hours of sleep daily	6 hours
Total hours of sleep in a week	42 hours
Number of available (useful) hours less the amount of sleep in a week	**126 hours**
Average wake up time to begin preparation for work	5.00 a.m.
Average time people get back home from work	9.00 p.m.
Total number of hours spent in work and work-related activities including transportation to-and-fro work	16 hours
Total number of work and work-related hours in a week (5-days)	**80 hours**
Work-related activities as a per cent of useful hours in a week	**63%**

APPENDIX B

THE SPIRITUALITY OF WORK

Charles is the human resources director of a leading multinational business. Although he enjoys what he is doing, recently, he has become conflicted. Why? His spiritual leader informed him that to serve God effectively, he should resign from his company and join his staff. While he would take a massive pay cut from his current salary if he joined the organisation, that was not the primary source of his confusion. His major confusion was, "Could he not serve God through his work?" As he thought about it, other questions arose in his mind, "Must he be a full-time staff of the ministry to serve God? What about the millions of people who are not in full-time ministry, are they outside the will and purpose of God?" He needs to give his spiritual leader an answer before the end of the month. Should he resign or not? How would you use the concept of this chapter to help him make the right decision?

There is a lot of confusion about the concept of work, especially among religious people. Some preachers even make people working feel guilty, like what Charles is currently going through. They use the concepts like, "You cannot serve God and mammon…The love of money is the root of all evil," to bring their people under the bondage of condemnation. They would rather have their people praying all day for a miracle and breakthroughs than working.

I will address the spirituality of work with three lessons:

God Worked

Have you ever wondered how God, the Almighty, introduced Himself to humanity? I call it the divine introduction. This is it: *"In the beginning, God created the heavens and the earth."*

God chose to introduce Himself through work, the creation of the heavens and earth. Of course, He could have introduced Himself differently, but He chose the creation story as His introduction.

Now you know why God rested after He finished creation. He expended energy! "And on the seventh day God ended His work which He had done, and He rested on the seventh day from all His work which He had done."

God rested because He worked.

And if God, the Omnipotent One, expended energy and worked, you cannot be exempted from working.

Key lesson: God worked!

If God worked, you too must work.

If the earth was established through work, there are no eternal exemption policies to working on earth!

God Gave Adam Work Before the Fall and the Curse

There are four primary institutions God gave humanity for holistic living: dominion, family, worship, and work.

Dominion deals with governance over the earth. It speaks to man's leadership ability. The institution of governance speaks to man's ability to control all of God's earthly creations. And man has largely exercised this ability to tame animals, harness the solar system's energies, and exploit earth's natural resources.

Family deals with relationships. God designed marriage and family to aid us in our pursuits of destiny.

Worship deals with man's relationship with God. Man was created to have fellowship with God and worship Him.

The final institution is work. God instituted work for Adam in the garden for the accomplishment of his purpose. We know that Adam's purpose was dominion. But the gateway was work—the garden. Put it this way: *tilling the ground is the gateway to dominating the earth.* Those who are called to dominate the earth must also learn to till the ground. Those who cannot till the ground cannot dominate the earth. To talk of dominion and to refuse to work to till the ground is to delude oneself.

Dominating the earth is a fantasy if we will not till the ground. Confessing dominion without committing to working is delusion, and I see many deluded religious people!

God gave these four institutions to man in man's purest state before sin entered the world. Thus, they are holy, consecrated, and relevant to man's ultimate destiny.

Work was given to man before the fall or before the curse. Therefore, it is a blessing and not a curse.

Key lesson: God instituted work.

If God instituted work, then work is spiritual.

If He instituted work before the fall and the curse, then work is a blessing and not a curse!

There Are No Undignified Jobs

I know we tend to rank professions in order of importance, but as long as the nature of work is not sinful, there are really no undignified jobs. Both blue and white-collar jobs can be a blessing.

Have you ever considered how God created man? He had to soil His hands with clay as the Master Potter. And if you look at the creation of the heavens and the earth, we see different career paths.

When God created the heavens, He made space exploration, space science, and space travel possible with all the careers associated with them.

When He said let there be light, He made the professions related to electricity generation, transmission, and distribution possible.

When He created the sea and marine life, He also made all the career options related to marine biology and aquatic life possible.

When He created dry land, He made careers in geology and other soil sciences possible.

When He made man, He made possible also all other careers related to man's needs. You can imagine how many they are.

When He planted a garden, He made the careers of florist, horticulturist, and farming possible.

When He put the man to sleep and took a rib to make the woman, guess the two professions that were birthed? Anaesthesiology and surgery (including reconstructive surgery).

When He clothed man in the Garden of Eden, He made possible every career related to the fashion industry.

We could go on.

There are no undignified professions, no undignified jobs, no undignified tasks. Some jobs might have been classified as menial jobs, but someone must do them. For example, someone has to remove your septic waste; another has to remove your trash; another has to clean the streets. The day they stop working is usually the day we learn to appreciate their roles.

I believe that if you look closely, you will find God as the first professional in every field of work that is not sinful or criminal.

Every work that is not sinful is spiritual, as you have seen. Take Joseph and Moses, for example.

Joseph's work was to provide food for the Israelites, while Moses was to deliver the Israelites from Egypt.

One had the title of Prime Minister and provider while the other prophet and deliverer.

One performed an economic miracle and the other supernatural miracles. But both were relevant. Without Joseph, there would not have been Moses. Had Joseph not provided for the people in famine, perhaps Moses would never have been born.

Your work might be like Joseph—to provide food for your family. You might be in farming, oil and gas, banking, IT or even politics. You may never preach a sermon or perform a miracle like Moses, but your work and purpose is as spiritual and important as that of the people in the Moses's camp.

There are many Josephs out there who do not see their roles as providers as important. But it is. Our calling as Josephs is to provide for people and not preach to them. The greatest message we preach as Josephs is the daily sacrifices we make to provide for our families and friends.

Don't try to become a Moses when you are supposed to work as a Joseph. If you are called to be a Joseph, celebrate your calling. Appreciate your contribution. But if you are called to be a Moses, you would know. The palace would not be comfortable for you. But please do not let anyone force you to make that decision.

So, Charles, you can serve God and fulfil your purpose as a Joseph. You need not resign your role to become a Moses.

I believe that if you look closely, you will find God as the first professional in every field of work that is not sinful or criminal.

REFERENCES

1. Bellah, R. N., Madsen, R., Sullivan, W. M., Swidler, A., & Tipton, S. M. (1985). Habits of the heart. New York: Harper & Row.
2. John W. Gardner (1995), Excellence: can we be equal and excellent too? New York: Norton
3. What UEFA records does Cristiano Ronaldo hold? / UEFA Champions League / UEFA.com

ABOUT THE AUTHOR

Dr. Ubah holds the prestigious Sloan Fellowship in Leadership and Strategy from the London Business School and has attended the Wharton Executive Education Programme on Strategic Thinking and Leadership for Growth. He is a leading leadership, strategy, and organisational transformation expert.

His core competencies are in personal and organisational transformation, leadership and people development including emotional intelligence and team effectiveness, change management design and implementation, strategy formulation and execution, and organisational performance optimisation.

He has facilitated training programmes for many reputable companies in Nigeria and across the globe with excellent ratings for his mode of delivery and the impact of his programmes.

He is the author of *The Alphabet of Leadership: The A-Z of Improving Your Leadership Effectiveness* and *The Difference: What Successful People Know and Do That Ordinary People Do Not.*

www.ingramcontent.com/pod-product-compliance
Lightning Source LLC
Chambersburg PA
CBHW032111040426
42337CB00040B/179